W9-DFE-032

CONTENTS

INTRODUCTION

People Who Said

NO

COURAGE
AGAINST
OPPRESSION

LAURA SCANDIFFIO

annick press
toronto + new york + vancouver

Edited by Catherine Marjoribanks
Designed by Sheryl Shapiro

Annick Press Ltd.

We acknowledge the support of the Canada Council for the Arts, the Ontario Arts Council, and the Government of Canada through the Canada Book Fund (CBF) for our publishing activities.

ONTARIO ARTS COUNCIL
CONSEIL DES ARTS DE L'ONTARIO

Cataloging in Publication

Scandiffio, Laura
    People who said no : courage against oppression / Laura Scandiffio.

Includes bibliographical references and index.
ISBN 978-1-55451-383-3 (bound).—ISBN 978-1-55451-382-6 (pbk.)

    1. Social reformers—Biography—Juvenile literature.
2. Dissenters—Biography—Juvenile literature. 3. Political
activists—Biography—Juvenile literature. I. Title.

HM881.S33 2012   j303.48'40922   C2012-900819-2

Distributed in Canada by:
Firefly Books Ltd.
66 Leek Crescent
Richmond Hill, ON
L4B 1H1

Published in the U.S.A. by Annick Press (U.S.) Ltd.
Distributed in the U.S.A. by:
Firefly Books (U.S.) Inc.
P.O. Box 1338
Ellicott Station
Buffalo, NY 14205

Printed in China

Visit us at: www.annickpress.com
Visit Laura Scandiffio at: www.laurascandiffio.com

TO all THOSE WHO, UNKNOWN TO MANY, STRUGGLE FOR JUSTICE,
aND WHOSE VISION OF a BETTER WORLD INSPIRES THEM TO aCT.
—L.S.

*A*s good citizens, we obey laws and follow rules. It makes living in harmony with one another possible. How else could a society work? Yet there have been times when good people have rebelled against authority, when they have refused to obey the law, when they have acted with bold defiance against those in power. Why did they do it?

To answer that question, ask yourself some others. What do you do when you know that the leaders and laws you're expected to obey are wrong? When they are racist, or persecute the powerless, or endanger the world, or instigate criminal acts you know are evil? And what if no one else is doing anything about it?

These are the questions the people in this book faced. They stood up against dictatorships, racism, the threat of nuclear destruction, and the persecution of helpless victims by the powerful—often putting their own lives at risk. Some acted alone. Others found strength in numbers, from the small resistance cell known as the White Rose in Nazi Germany to the thousands-strong people's uprising in Egypt in 2011.

There are many different ways to say no to injustice. It may mean challenging unfair laws in court, or simply speaking out against wrongdoing when people in power want to silence all protest. The tools of rebellion may be public demonstrations, the printed word or, more recently, the Internet. Rosa Parks, by refusing to give up her seat on a segregated bus, used the strategy of passive resistance, peacefully disobeying a law she knew was wrong and, by refusing, challenging and exposing it for the world to see. Passive resistance was embraced by Mahatma Gandhi, who struggled against the British for India's independence and for the dignity of its minorities. Gandhi, like Martin Luther King Jr., inspired a number of the people whose stories are told here.

Some, like Rosa Parks, are famous; others are less well known. Helen Suzman may not be as famous as her fellow anti-apartheid crusaders Nelson Mandela and Desmond Tutu, but her story is important, too. Although she could have lived a life of privilege, turning a blind eye to the injustice done to others around her, she refused to do so. For decades, she stood steadfast and alone, shining a light on the evils of apartheid and refusing to be silenced.

Many of the people in this book did not start out as heroes of resistance. They were bystanders, accepting or sometimes even approving of the status quo. But they reached a turning point, a moment of clarity when their consciences would not let them go on as they had before. Oscar Romero, the conservative archbishop of El Salvador, at first stood by while his government persecuted the poor, but the murder of a priest who championed peasants' rights changed everything. From then on, he dedicated his life to protecting the poor and oppressed, regardless of the danger. Andrei Sakharov helped to create Russia's first thermonuclear bomb. Only later did he fully realize the horrible implications of his creation and become a crusader against nuclear weapons, and a champion of world peace. Some were drawn by chance into a cause and never looked back, like Aung San Suu Kyi, whose visit to her dying mother brought her into the midst of a fight for democracy in Burma that continues today.

These seven instances of "saying no" are only a handful

of examples, among countless others, of people who have stood up to injustice around the world and through time. Their courage and vision—and their firm conviction that beliefs must be translated into action—continue to inspire us. Like circles of light in the surrounding darkness, they prove that one person can make a tremendous difference, by making the world better for humankind and by inspiring new generations to recognize and oppose injustice.

Author's Note

For these stories, I drew on factual accounts, biographies, and memoirs written by the people themselves. Each story is based closely on true events. However, in retelling them, I have adapted some conversations or scenes to dramatize the person's struggle.

THE WHITE ROSE

Alone Against Hitler

Munich, Germany, 1942

Sophie Scholl pushed the last of the envelopes into the mailbox and let the lid fall. The noise made her jump. As she turned away and hurried home through the dark streets, she knew nothing would ever be the same. She had committed treason. Her country was at war, and she was doing all she could to help bring down her own government. She—and people she loved—could die if anyone found out.

Sophie glanced over her shoulder every other moment, but she was strangely calm. It had been growing a long time, her certainty that she must act and no longer stand by out of fear, as others did. Germany was in the hands of a dictator. Now she and her brother Hans were both "traitors" according to the laws of Nazi Germany. But how can a good person obey laws that are evil?

"Think for yourselves," Sophie's parents had always encouraged their five children. "Don't follow the herd." Their words came back to her now, but with a pang. She was twenty-one years old—it wasn't so long ago that she'd still been a carefree girl at home, never dreaming of defiance, much less treason.

THE THRILL OF A NEW ERA

Growing up in the small city of Ulm, Sophie noticed that her father wasn't like most other parents. Robert Scholl didn't always agree with the majority, and he was unafraid to say so. He hated violence, and during World War I he had refused to fight—an unpopular choice in a country full of flag-waving patriots dreaming of military victories. Instead he'd driven ambulances and tended the wounded. He'd met and married soft-spoken Magdalene, a Red Cross nurse, while they served in the same hospital. Sophie's mother was calmer than headstrong Robert.

The hero of young Sophie's life was her older brother, Hans. It was easy for anyone to fall under Hans's spell. Tall and dark-haired, he was often called a born leader. He never worried about being like everyone else. Yet he was also restless, always craving action. Sophie was different—quieter and more thoughtful, but also unpredictable. And she could be very determined.

Sophie was not yet twelve when the Nazi Party, led by Adolf Hitler, came to power in Germany. Across the country, young people were caught up in the excitement of the new era he promised them. Nazi flags hung from windows, and people crowded into the streets to watch parading troops waving banners, singing, and marching in unison to the beat of drums. They cheered the dramatic speeches of Hitler, whose voice rose to a pitch that worked crowds into a frenzy.

SAFER RICHER STRONGER

Like so many of their friends, Sophie and Hans were impressed and longed to join what seemed like a wonderful celebration. It looked as though the Nazis really were making the country safer, richer, stronger. Why then, Sophie wondered, did her father close the blinds to block the sight of the flags, and turn off the radio when Hitler spoke? On a family hike along the river, Sophie peppered her father with questions. Couldn't he see the government's victories? "After all," Hans broke in, "Hitler kept his promise to get rid of unemployment."

"No one denies that," their father snapped. "But don't ask about his methods! He started up the weapons industry. He's building soldiers' barracks. Do you know where that will lead?"

HITLER'S RISE TO POWER

A former soldier and failed artist, Adolf Hitler achieved dramatic and rapid success as a political leader in Germany. Hitler was bitter about Germany's defeat in World War I (1914–1918), and believed that the German soldiers had been betrayed by their government when it surrendered. After the war he joined a new, small political group in Munich, and by 1921 he was its leader. The National Socialist German Workers' Party soon became known as the Nazi Party. Hitler now found his particular talent: he was an angry, fiery public speaker, and he could rally crowds to follow him. He had a genius for tapping into people's fears and resentments.

The Nazis blamed Germany's government for the massive unemployment that plagued Germany in the 1930s. They spread the belief that the country needed a strong government to defend Germany's interests. Hitler promised to solve Germany's problems quickly and to restore pride to a nation humiliated by defeat.

German dictator Adolf Hitler roused crowds of supporters with his dramatic speeches.

The Nazis triumphed in the 1932 elections. In the following year, Hitler rapidly set up a dictatorship, granting himself absolute powers and making opposition to his government illegal. He became known as the *Führer*, which means "leader," and he began to put his beliefs into practice, especially the idea that the Germans were a superior race and had a natural right to rule others. He blamed Germany's Jewish people for many problems, and passed laws to persecute them.

Hitler built up a powerful army, and in 1939 Germany invaded Poland, igniting World War II. Throughout the war, the Nazis' attacks on Jews escalated, resulting in the Holocaust, the mass murder of Jews and other persecuted people.

At dinner they debated politics, but Sophie could see that Hans had stopped listening to their father. She cringed when the meal ended in shouting.

TAKING SIDES

The Nazis were keen to capture young people's loyalty, and they set up clubs for children and teens. In 1933, fifteen-year-old Hans defied his father's objections and joined the Hitler Youth. Sophie's jaw dropped at the sight of her brother striding boldly through the door in uniform.

Her father exploded. "Your Führer—he's the Pied Piper, leading you foolish children down a path to destruction!"

From then on, an icy silence descended whenever the two were in the same room. Sophie silently agreed with Hans—their father's suspicions made no sense—and she stubbornly joined the German Girls' League, the Hitler

Bearing Nazi flags, Hitler Youth members march at a rally.

Youth's female counterpart. Her father shook his head, but there was no outburst this time. "Even my wise child … " he muttered, his voice trailing off. Life at home became tense.

Hans was quickly put in charge of a Hitler Youth squad. He tackled the job with spirit, playing the guitar and teaching his squad all the foreign folk songs he knew. "Stop it," Hitler Youth authorities told him. "Those songs aren't German!" Hans resented their interference. "Why can't they let anyone think for themselves?" he grumbled to Sophie. "So many rules: what to say, what to read, who can be your friend!"

He seemed to forget his irritation when, in 1935, he received a huge honor: he was chosen by the Ulm branch to carry the Party flag at the Nazis' annual rally in Nuremberg. Sophie's friends gushed to her about the event, and she began to share their excitement. Their father refused to speak to Hans—which only fired up his determination to go.

Sophie knew the gatherings in Nuremberg were always spectacular. Enormous military parades, impassioned speeches, each night ablaze with searchlights and torches—all designed to impress everyone with the Nazis' power. She waited eagerly for Hans to return triumphant, full of exciting stories. To her surprise, however, he was quiet when he came back, his eyes downcast. He didn't want to talk about the rally, muttering only that the crowds there were "mindless." Something had changed him, and his depressed mood worried Sophie. But she could not draw him out. Why had he stopped confiding in her?

SEEDS OF DOUBT

In fact, Sophie was having second thoughts, too. At first, she'd enjoyed the activities at the German Girls' League. But their teachings bothered her. Sophie wanted to go to

A sign in 1930s Ulm warns, "Jews are not desirable in Ulm."

university, but the leaders said a girl's only job was to become a wife and mother. She was also upset that her friends Luise and Anneliese couldn't join because they were Jewish. She stubbornly stayed friends with them and kept inviting them home. But over the past year, ever since the Nazis had passed their new anti-Jewish laws, things had changed radically for Sophie's Jewish friends. They were no longer allowed in movie theaters, swimming pools, or parks. Soon they would be forced into a separate school.

Whatever feelings were simmering inside Hans, they soon boiled over. Arriving home late one night, he stormed into his room and slammed the door behind him. Bewildered, Sophie sought out her older sister, who told her what had happened.

Hans had helped the boys in his troop design their own banner, decorated with a griffin. He'd let one twelve-year-old carry it when they lined up for inspection. An adult leader took one look and glared down at the boy: "Hand that over! You can't have a banner of your own. Use the one in the manual." The man grabbed the boy's arm roughly, wrenching the flag free.

"Stop bullying him!" Hans shouted. Impulsively he rushed between them, and in the struggle he punched the man's chin. Hans was immediately stripped of his rank, in front of everyone.

The incident seemed to ignite rebellion in Hans. He kept on leading a group of friends from the squad in a club of their own that ignored Hitler Youth rules and traveled without permission. Sophie knew very well that the Nazis didn't like teens forming clubs other than the Hitler Youth, whose members could be controlled. Most other youth groups were now illegal. She was afraid for Hans.

Sophie's own misgivings became harder to ignore. A teacher disappeared suddenly. Rumors spread that he had been taken to a "concentration camp." His mother came to visit Sophie's parents, and Sophie listened as Magdalene asked what he'd done. "Nothing," the teacher's mother sobbed. "He just wasn't a Nazi … That was his crime."

Sophie was gripped by a strange feeling, as if they had all been living in a beautiful house, but now knew that something evil and shameful lurked in the cellar. Something told her that Hans felt it, too. One day he broke the stalemate with their father.

"What's a concentration camp?" he asked.

Robert Scholl flinched, and Sophie watched anxiously as Hans and her father stared at each other. Then her father calmly told them what he knew. The Nazis were rounding up anyone who didn't fit into their vision of a new Germany—communists, Gypsies, Jews, people with disabilities—and taking them to camps surrounded by barbed wire. He wasn't sure what happened there, but they were never seen again.

HOW COULD THIS HAPPEN?

"How could this happen?" Sophie cried.

Robert sighed. "In times of trouble, people will listen to

promises and temptations and not ask who offers them." He put a hand on his son's shoulder.

The angry tension that had filled the house seemed to melt away. From then on, they began to trust and depend on one another more than ever. The family became like an island in a stormy sea.

A FIST ON THE DOOR

In the spring of 1937, Sophie said good-bye to her brother. Hans was keen to begin university, but like all young men his age, he would first have to work for six months in the new national labor service. He would build roads, and then be drafted into the army for two years. Sophie felt left behind, and their letters were a lifeline.

That November, while Hans was away at his military training, the doorbell rang at the Scholls' house one evening. Before anyone could answer, a fist pounded on the door. "Gestapo! Open up!"

Sophie watched from the staircase as her father opened the door. Two men in gray overcoats stood outside. *They've come for Father*, was Sophie's first panicked thought. But the men were not interested in Robert Scholl. One of them pointed at Sophie and motioned to her to come down the stairs. It took several seconds for her to realize the truth. They were there to arrest *her*. Within moments, Sophie, her sister Inge, and brother Werner were being herded into a waiting car, while their parents watched anxiously.

At Gestapo headquarters, all three were put into separate cells. Sophie had no idea what would happen. Then the questions began, all about Hans. Whom did he spend time with? What about this youth group he used to lead— where did they go, what did they do? Sophie had little to tell and nothing

THE GESTAPO
HITLER'S WATCHDOGS

The Nazis' special political police, the Gestapo (short for "Secret State Police" in German), rooted out any opponents they imagined might threaten Nazi power. It became unsafe to criticize Hitler at work or even among friends. A casual remark or a lack of enthusiasm about the Nazis could land a person in trouble. Gestapo agents had the power to arrest people they suspected and hold them in "protective custody" for as long as they liked. The Gestapo relied on tip-offs from common Germans who, eager to show their loyalty to the Führer, reported on neighbors, co-workers, and teachers.

Under the Nazis, people were often stopped and searched by Gestapo and other security police. Fear of arrest was widespread.

to hide, and she was quickly released. Her sister and brother followed soon after.

But for Hans it was a different story. Sophie found out that Gestapo agents had barged into the army barracks where Hans was training and led him away in handcuffs. He was under arrest for activities with his "illegal" youth group. Now he was in solitary confinement, waiting for his trial. Sophie couldn't visit him or even send him a Christmas package. She could only imagine how he must be living, alone, in the shadow of what was coming.

Five weeks passed before Hans was released. In the end, the judge was lenient: Hans was, after all, a "pure" German, a young person who had made mistakes but would do better in the future.

Hans put on a forced cheerfulness. "I'm going to work hard and make you proud of me," he told his parents.

Sophie followed his lead and even cracked jokes about her "arrest." But at night she had vivid, frightening dreams. In her mind, she had reached a turning point, and one thing was very clear—the world the Nazis had made was rotten and unjust to its core.

People Who Said No

SILENT DISSENT

In 1939, with Germany's invasion of Poland, the country was at war. All around Sophie, people displayed patriotic zeal, but she felt angry. At eighteen, she began her own labor service. Making weapons on an assembly line, she was constantly reminded of the madness of the war her country had started.

Through it all, she clung to her dream of going to university. In May 1942, shortly after her twenty-first birthday, Sophie arrived at last at the University of Munich, where Hans was already studying medicine. Very soon, though, she felt like a misfit. The student union was full of enthusiastic Nazis. Sophie became careful never to share her inner thoughts, even with the friends she made.

Her brother's arrest had convinced her of the truth. The Nazis proclaimed that they acted for the good of the German people, but they were actually enslaving them, taking away their freedoms, and crushing all the Party's opponents. People said it was everyone's duty to support the government during wartime, but wasn't it a greater duty to oppose an evil regime? And yet, she was surrounded by people who would gladly turn her in for even hinting at what she believed.

OPPOSE THE EVIL REGIME

THE COURAGE TO ACT

Weeks after Sophie arrived at the university, something extraordinary happened. Spotting a sheet of printed paper on the floor of a lecture room, she picked it up and glanced at the words: "It is certain that today every honest German is ashamed of his government." For a moment she was breathless. It was as if someone had printed her own thoughts.

Her eyes scanned the rest of the page. Don't wait for someone else to act, the writer implored. Resist! The note ended with a plea: "Please make as many copies of this leaflet as you can and pass them on."

Sophie stuffed the paper into her pocket, her hand shaking. She glanced around to see if anyone had noticed her reading it. The words echoed in her head; they sounded like a familiar voice. She headed for Hans's apartment. Her uneasiness grew along the way.

Sophie smoothed out the leaflet and placed it before Hans. Did he know anything about it?

His reaction chilled her. "Better not ask who wrote it. It could put the person's life in danger."

BETTER NOT ASK

That's when she knew. The familiar voice was Hans's. He denied writing it at first, then, taking the paper from her hand, nodded.

Bit by bit, Sophie dragged out the whole truth. Hans hadn't acted alone. His good friend from military training, Alex Schmorell, had supplied a typewriter and helped Hans make copies on a duplicating machine. They had hand-cranked out a hundred or so leaflets, and mailed them to random addresses in the city directory.

"What are you trying to do?" Sophie cried. "Don't you see the danger you're putting yourself in?"

"That's the problem," Hans answered, growing heated. "Everyone's too afraid to act, locked up in their own little prison." Sophie had to remind him to lower his voice.

"I started thinking," he went on more quietly, "what if there are others who feel just like I do? But they're invisible to me, because no one says anything. What if I could reach them? Ignite their good impulses?" Hans's eyes were flashing now. "If we roused enough people, a wave of resistance could grow across the country. It could knock the Nazis from power!"

The addresses weren't quite random, he explained. He

and Alex had targeted educated people. If teachers, scientists, and doctors could be swayed against the Nazis, their opinions would influence others.

All Sophie's objections died in an instant. "I want to help," she said. "Please let me."

A SECRET LIFE BEGINS

Two other trusted friends joined them: Christoph Probst, Alex's quiet best friend, who trailed him like a shadow, and Willi Graf. Like Hans, Willi had been arrested in his teens for belonging to a youth group that criticized the Nazis. Sophie felt she could trust the serious-looking Willi right away. "I believe he never says anything," she marveled, "unless he's ready to back up his words with his whole being."

Together Hans and Alex wrote a second leaflet. This one laid out the blunt facts of Nazi evildoing against the Jews. All

Hans Scholl, Sophie Scholl, and Christoph Probst in the summer of 1942

were guilty if they stood by and did nothing. Now that the war had shown the Nazis for what they truly were, "it must be the sole and first duty, the holiest duty of every German to destroy these beasts."

Sophie helped print and put the leaflets into envelopes and snuck out at night to stuff them into mailboxes. She was now leading a double life—a student during the day, waging a secret rebellion at night. And she was afraid. But anything was better than living with the shame of doing nothing.

She had good reason to be fearful. Someone sent a copy of the first leaflet to the Gestapo. Agents enlisted a language expert to analyze it and form a profile of the writer. The expert reported that it was the work of a young, romantic idealist. He guessed the author was not a loner, but part of a group. A Gestapo search for this "idealist" began.

STOPPING THE WAR MACHINE

In July, the Scholls' schemes came to a halt. Hans and his friends were ordered back into the army to take part in Hitler's invasion of Russia. Working as medics among the wounded, Hans and Alex saw Jews and Russian prisoners of war abused by German guards. They were horrified by the misery the Nazis had brought to Poland and Russia. By the time they returned to Munich in the fall, they had reached a radical conclusion. There was only one way to stop the Nazis: Germany must lose the war.

The message of their third leaflet demanded action. "Sabotage in armaments-works and war-factories. Sabotage all meetings, assemblies, and demonstrations organized by the National Socialist Party," it urged. Each person could strike a blow; together, a thousand acts would cripple "the war machine."

The leaflets were now signed "the White

Medical student Wilhelm ("Willi") Graf was strongly opposed to Nazism from its beginnings.

Rose." White stood for peace and neutrality from any political group, but beyond that the name was deliberately mysterious. The Gestapo came to new conclusions in their hunt: they were dealing with a large organization, possibly working with the countries at war with Germany. But the location and identity of the authors continued to baffle them.

Sophie lived in constant suspense. It amazed her that they hadn't been caught yet. *It could happen anytime*, she thought. The accusing finger would point at her, but when and where? In class, or one day on the street?

"And if we're arrested?" she asked Hans.

"If any one of us is caught, we say we acted alone—so the others have a chance."

Hans seemed so fearless, but instead of reassuring Sophie his confidence frightened her more. Was his judgment sound? Willi was always pulling him back from taking unnecessary risks.

A NEW ALLY, A DANGEROUS ENEMY

Hans was obviously frustrated. Their call for sabotage was a radical leap, but what impact had it produced? Nothing!

"We need a better writer," Hans announced.

The city of Ulm, Germany, home of the Scholl family

"Kurt Huber!" Sophie cried out immediately. Professor Huber's lectures at the university were so popular that she had once snuck in to listen. Huber even dared to criticize the Nazis! They decided to pay the professor an evening visit.

Huber listened in silence to Hans and Alex's stories of horrors in Russia, his face stern. He agreed to write the next leaflet, and he didn't mince words. The new leaflet made a blunt call to Germans, imploring them to act now or face doom: "Hitler cannot win the war; he can only prolong it." Huber asked Germans if they wanted to be forever hated by the rest of the world. He called for "freedom of speech, freedom of religion, the protection of individual citizens from the arbitrary will of criminal regimes of violence." This time, the group made nearly ten thousand copies of their plea.

Lugging a suitcase full of leaflets, Sophie made a dangerous trek by train to post their message in Augsburg, Stuttgart, and Ulm. It was risky: the trains were closely patrolled by Gestapo, who could search passengers at any time. Willi had already made a perilous journey over the winter holidays, mailing leaflets from different cities to keep the location of the White Rose a secret.

The Gestapo were now seriously alarmed. At their Munich headquarters, they created a special task force to find the culprits immediately, with agent Robert Mohr in charge. Another language expert declared that the author of the latest leaflet was an academic. Other experts determined that the paper, envelopes, and stamps had all been bought in Munich. Mohr ordered that all post offices be on the lookout for anyone buying a large quantity of stamps.

RUNNING RISKS

Hans was getting more reckless. Without telling the others, he and Alex snuck through the city one night, painting graffiti on buildings —"Hitler the Mass Murderer" and "Freedom" in bold letters a meter (three feet) high. Sophie knew such

actions directed too much attention to Munich. But as always when faced with Hans's audacity, she lost any urge to scold him. She made him promise to take her next time. If he was facing danger, she wanted to be there, too.

The strain of their underground life was showing. A meeting with Huber turned into a furious argument, and Huber stormed out. Christoph, who was married with young children, began to hint that he'd had enough. Hans was sure he was being tailed in the streets. In fact, Mohr and the Gestapo weren't that close yet, but the anti-Hitler graffiti had narrowed their search. They ordered university officials to watch out for anything suspicious.

Hans and Sophie persisted, printing thousands of copies of their sixth leaflet. Hans went out to buy postage stamps as usual, but as soon as he left the post office, the clerk reported the large purchase to the Gestapo.

Back at the apartment, Hans proposed they drop leaflets around the university. "That's too risky—it's crazy," Willi protested. But Hans wouldn't listen. He looked imploringly at Sophie. She agreed to help him with his plan.

A FINAL VENTURE

On the morning of February 18, 1943, Hans and Sophie carried a suitcase stuffed with leaflets onto the campus. The lobby of the main building was empty; all the students were inside the lecture hall. They hurried through, dropping leaflets as they went. Despite Willi's concerns, Sophie felt confident they could empty the suitcase and get out before the lecture finished. They hauled the suitcase up the grand central stairs. At the top, Hans placed a stack of leaflets on the marble railing.

All morning, Sophie had been filled with nervous excitement. She glanced at the pile and, on a sudden impulse, pushed them over the edge with a sweep of her hand. In the same moment, the lecture hall doors opened and students flooded out. All faces turned upward to the leaflets floating

down like huge snowflakes. Jakob Schmid, a university porter, looked up, too, straight into Sophie's startled face.

"Stop where you are!" he shouted, running up the stairs. Sophie, still holding the suitcase, dashed into an empty classroom, but Schmid was on her heels.

Hans made no move to run. He couldn't leave Sophie. He'd have to stand his ground and deny everything.

Robert Mohr and his Gestapo force arrived quickly. "Why were you carrying an empty suitcase?" Mohr asked Sophie.

"I was going home for a few days and was going to bring back some clean laundry." She answered so calmly, and it sounded plausible.

Mohr looked puzzled. What could these polite students have to do with the treasonous White Rose? He glanced at Schmid, wondering if he had grabbed the wrong people.

Hans suddenly realized that he had the draft of another leaflet, written by Christoph, in his pocket. While the Gestapo were picking up the scattered leaflets, he quietly tore it to bits. An agent glanced up and spotted him. Mohr quickly fit the pieces together.

"A stranger gave it to me," Hans told him.

"So why did you try to destroy it?" Mohr demanded.

"I was worried it would make me look suspicious."

Mohr stared at Hans, still unsure. "Handcuff them," he said at last. He led Hans and Sophie through the crowd of staring students and drove them to Gestapo headquarters.

IN THE HANDS OF THE GESTAPO

Hans and Sophie were put in separate rooms. *Remember,* Sophie told herself, *if it comes to that, I say I acted alone.* But she still hoped to deny everything. Sophie stuck to her story about going home, and Mohr could not trip her up. Her hopes rose.

Outside her interrogation room, everything was unraveling for Hans. Agents searched his apartment and found piles of stamps and envelopes. They had also arrested a friend of theirs at the lecture hall. Sophie had never confided in her, but she revealed everything odd she'd seen or suspected. At 4:00 a.m., Hans, exhausted by hours of nonstop questioning, was confronted with this evidence. He decided the time had come to take the blame upon himself. Maybe he could still save Sophie.

HIGH TREASON

Mohr slapped down Hans's written confession on the table before Sophie. Her head spun as she read it, and all hope drained away. "Yes, I helped him," she said quietly. But she insisted there was no one else.

The Gestapo, however, followed their own tips. Willi Graf was arrested the same day, Christoph Probst the next. Endless questioning produced nothing against Willi, who stubbornly refused to confess or give anyone away, but handwriting samples identified Christoph as the author of the draft in Hans's pocket. A wanted poster was printed for Alex, who now raced from one hiding place to another. Professor Huber was arrested at home two days later.

Nazi officials ordered that the White Rose be dealt with swiftly and ruthlessly. They still had no idea how big the group was. Any remaining members, they determined, must be terrified into silence by the fate of the prime culprits. On February 21, Sophie was called out of her jail cell and told she was being charged with high treason. She was handed the formal charge, which she read silently. Then she turned it over and wrote one word on the back: "Freedom." Before she returned to her cell, she was told her trial would take place in the morning. Hans and Christoph received the same dire news.

A lawyer stopped by Sophie's cell, saying he had been assigned to defend them all. Bored and impatient, he clearly intended to do little to help. "I will share the same fate as my brother," Sophie told him. "If he has to die, so will I."

ON TRIAL

Sophie woke early in the morning, and was waiting when agents arrived at her cell to take her to the special "People's Court," hastily set up for the trial. She, Hans, and Christoph were made to stand behind a railing, an armed guard on each side. Roland Freisler, a ruthless Nazi judge, had been summoned from Berlin to preside. There would be no jury, no witnesses for the defense, and no family or friends allowed inside. Most of the spectators staring coldly at the three students were Nazi officials and troopers.

Judge Freisler strode in, and the evidence against the students was quickly presented; Christoph's draft was read aloud, as were snatches of the leaflets. Freisler asked each of them to stand and state his or her involvement.

Roland Freisler, president of the People's Court, which dealt with acts of opposition against the Nazi state

Hans got to his feet, but as soon as he began to speak Freisler interrupted, shouting and bullying him. It became obvious the trial was his showcase to humiliate and torment Nazi enemies. Sophie watched Hans, so pale and haggard, standing upright in the face of insults hurled at him. She admired him more than ever. When her turn came, she was amazed by her own calm. She defended what she had done in a clear voice, repenting nothing.

As soon as she sat down, the prosecutor demanded the death penalty for all three. For the first time in the rapid-fire trial, the judge paused. "Any last words?" he asked.

Hans stood again. "I ask for mercy for Christoph Probst, who has young children—"

"Shut up!" Freisler roared.

One by one, they were told to stand, while Freisler read out the verdicts. Sophie got to her feet first. She was found guilty of treason and sentenced to death. She listened without flinching. Christoph received the same verdict and sentence, as did Hans. When Freisler had finished, there was silence, which Hans broke in a loud voice that startled the whole court.

"Today you will hang us, but soon you will be standing where I stand now!"

People Who Said No

A commotion in the back of the court made Sophie turn. Her father had just barged inside the courtroom, followed by her mother and younger brother, Werner. Hearing the verdict, her mother nearly collapsed.

"Get rid of them!" Freisler bellowed at the guards.

Handcuffs were snapped around Sophie's wrists, and she was hauled away with her brother and Christoph.

Robert Scholl was begging any lawyer who would listen to help him appeal the verdict. Werner Scholl, allowed to pass because of his army uniform, pushed through the crowd, and for a brief moment, touched his brother's and sister's hands. "Stay strong," Hans told him before they were parted.

"LONG LIVE FREEDOM"

Sophie's parents followed them to the prison and persuaded a guard to give them a few moments with their children. Hans was brought in first, his face strained. He didn't want to talk about what was coming, but thanked his parents for all they had done for him. "I have no hate for anyone any-more," he said. "I have put all that behind me."

His father searched for words to comfort him. "You'll go down in history," he said. "There is another justice than this."

Sophie came next. She put on a brave face for what she knew was a last meeting. Her mother offered her candy, which she took. "I've not eaten any lunch," she said, and smiled. She told her parents she was proud of what she and Hans had done. "We took everything upon ourselves," she said. "What will happen will cause waves." Guards cut the visit short, and Sophie returned to her cell, where she burst into tears.

No visitors came for Christoph Probst. His wife was still in the hospital after the birth of their third child. She didn't know yet about his trial.

At 4:00 p.m. Sophie was taken to a prison office, where the trial prosecutor was waiting for her behind a large table. There would be no mercy, he said in a cold voice. Justice, and the death sentence, would be carried out in one hour. Nazi officials were afraid a public execution might start a riot. It was better to announce their deaths afterward.

Only then did Sophie know how little time she had left. One hour in her cell. The prison chaplain visited her, and was kind. She prayed and, again, she was amazed by the calm she felt inside.

When the guard arrived at her door, Sophie Scholl walked calmly from her cell to the guillotine chamber. Her execution took place in seconds. Hans and Christoph followed, one after the other. Just before the blade descended on Hans Scholl, he cried out loudly:

"Long live freedom!"

The Gestapo continued to hunt down anyone connected to the White Rose. Upon his capture, Alex wasn't told that Hans and Sophie had confessed and been executed, and he tried to save them by taking full responsibility. Alex, Willi, and Huber were executed in the months that followed. Many other friends and helpers were imprisoned.

COURAGE REMEMBERED

Today, memorials at the university in Munich honor the White Rose; schools and city streets are named after the

members. "We will not be silent," they wrote in one of their leaflets. "We are your bad conscience. The White Rose will not leave you in peace!"

It can't be known how many people their campaign inspired to defy the Nazis in secret, but it's estimated that fewer than one percent of Germans actively resisted the Nazi regime. Those who did fought a lonely battle, following their conscience while surrounded by people who would betray them or were too afraid to help. Although a few brave people tried, no resistance effort toppled Hitler from power. The armies of the Allies (led by England, the United States, and Russia) finally defeated Hitler and his regime. The White Rose's lone stance against tyranny makes their courage, and that of the few other German resisters, all the more inspiring.

A memorial to the White Rose at Munich's university combines scattered leaflets with photos of the members. Clockwise from top left, Alexander Schmorell, Sophie Scholl, and Hans Scholl.

Rosa Parks

Bus Ride to Freedom

Montgomery, Alabama, 1955

"They've messed with the wrong one now!"

The girl's high voice reached Rosa's ears through the noisy crowd. Rosa almost smiled, as she nervously mounted the steps of City Hall. She understood what the girl meant. Here she was, so prim and respectable in her neat suit and gloves—she didn't look like a criminal. She sure didn't *feel* like a criminal. And yet, according to the laws of Montgomery, she was. Simply because she wouldn't give up her seat on the bus.

Now they were chanting her name. *Rosa! Rosa!* All eyes were on her. She was about to learn what it meant to be a symbol to millions of people. They would always ask her: Did you plan it? Did it just happen? The answer wasn't so simple.

HARSH LESSONS

As a child, Rosa was shy and sickly, but beamed when she was praised by her grandfather or a teacher. Her father was a traveling carpenter who disappeared from her life when she was five. Her mother had to travel for her teaching job, so Rosa grew up in her grandparents' home in the small town of Pine Level, Alabama.

In Pine Level, Rosa learned early that black children like her and her little brother, Sylvester, didn't mix with white children. They even went to separate schools. Grandmother warned Rosa not to talk back to any whites, children or adults. But her grandfather, so light-skinned he could be mistaken for a white man, liked to shock white neighbors by shaking their hands and calling them by their first names, something blacks never did. Rosa couldn't figure out how he got away with his "sass," as it was called. He was proud and taught Rosa never to put up with bad treatment from anyone.

"SEPARATE BUT EQUAL"

Slavery was abolished throughout the U.S. at the end of the Civil War in 1865, but the separation of whites and blacks (segregation) remained a way of life in many southern states, such as Alabama and Louisiana. Separate theaters, restaurants, and schools kept blacks and whites from encountering each other as equals.

In 1892, Homer Plessy, who had a black great-grandmother, was arrested for riding in a whites-only railcar in Louisiana. His case went to the Supreme Court. Plessy argued that separate railcars were illegal under the Constitution's Fourteenth Amendment, which guaranteed equal protection of the law to everyone. In *Plessy v. Ferguson*, the Supreme Court ruled in 1896 that racial segregation did not violate anyone's rights, as long as facilities were "separate but equal."

That ruling gave southern states the means of passing laws that would enforce segregation in every aspect of life.

This bus terminal in Memphis, Tennessee, provided a "whites-only" waiting room.

By the time she was six, Rosa realized a terrible truth: slavery may have ended long ago, but she was not free. She heard stories of groups of whites who disguised themselves in white hoods and robes and terrorized the black people of Pine Level after dark. They called themselves the Ku Klux Klan (KKK). Grandfather kept a loaded shotgun at his side all night.

"I don't know how long it would last if they came breaking in here," he told Rosa, "but I'm getting the first one who comes through the door." Rosa curled up next to his chair by the fire. *Whatever happens*, she thought, *I want to see it; I don't want to be caught asleep.* For comfort, Rosa thought about her favorite Bible stories, especially the one about Moses standing up to Pharaoh, demanding that he let the children of Israel go free. And she remembered that there were kind white people, too, like the old lady who took her fishing at the creek and would even visit her grandparents and chat for hours.

In 1920s Virginia, Ku Klux Klan members prowl at night.

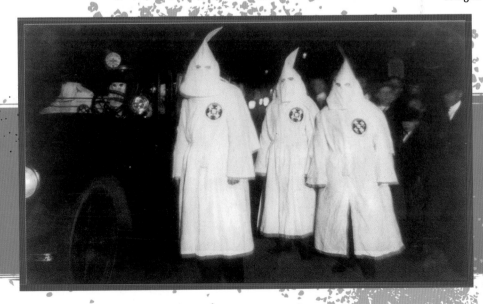

AIMING HIGHER

Rosa's mother and grandfather wanted her to have a good education, but in Pine Level the black elementary schools didn't go beyond early grades. Rosa would have to go live with relatives in Montgomery, the state capital.

Rosa was dazzled by Montgomery, the biggest city she'd ever seen. As she walked alongside her mother, she stared at the honking cars and tall buildings. Passing a water fountain, she stopped for a drink in the heat of the afternoon. Her mother anxiously tugged her sleeve and pointed at the sign above the fountain. "Whites" it read. Rosa hadn't seen it. Her mother nodded toward a fountain farther along the street, older-looking, with a "Colored" sign above it. *So we don't even drink the same water*, Rosa thought. *I wonder if the white water tastes different?*

A "colored" drinking fountain outside a court-house in 1930s North Carolina

Rosa loved her new school. The teachers were white women from the northern states who'd come to Alabama to educate black girls. They told Rosa to aim high, that she was

COLORED

a person with dignity who should treat herself with respect and insist that others do the same. It was like hearing her grandfather's voice. The teachers frowned on the girls dancing or wearing jewelry, but Rosa didn't mind. She'd always been a bit serious about life, too.

Rosa's school closed when she was in the eighth grade. Many white people in Montgomery had no sympathy for the northern teachers giving black children so much education, and they had never been welcome. Rosa had to forget schooling soon anyway, to take care of her mother, who became so ill she couldn't teach. By sixteen, Rosa was working as a seamstress and cleaning homes part-time, paying the bills for her sick mother.

FACING UP TO RACISM

Life began to change for Rosa when she met Raymond Parks, a young barber. Raymond often told Rosa how outraged he felt—so few black people were registered to vote, so many innocent blacks were arrested for crimes they obviously didn't commit. He wanted to change things. He joined the National Association for the Advancement of Colored People (NAACP), a group that helped blacks register to vote and fought prejudice. Raymond's passion for black rights opened Rosa's eyes. They married, and he encouraged Rosa to finish high school.

During World War II, Rosa Parks got a job on a local military base, where blacks and whites worked and even ate lunch together. Rosa would ride a shuttle bus around the base, sitting next to white co-workers; but going home on the city bus in Montgomery, she and all the other black passengers had to sit in the back. If all those seats were taken, blacks had to stand, even if there were empty seats in the front section reserved for whites. It was humiliating, and worse, she often had to put up with the driver's racist remarks.

Rosa thought about her brother, now in the army fighting for democracy in Europe. Yet at home he couldn't vote. She decided to get registered herself.

On one of her trips to register, she had a menacing encounter with a bus driver. Some drivers were meaner than others, and they made black riders pay their fare at the front, then step off and walk around to the back door to get on. Sometimes they'd even drive off before the person could board again. As soon as Rosa mounted the steps, she knew she'd come across a mean one. He was big and rough-looking, and he glared at her. The back of the bus was crowded—she'd never be able to get past the people on the back steps to board—so she paid and walked to the back. The driver called after her to get off and board from the back door.

"It's too crowded," Rosa explained.

"Get off *my* bus," the driver shouted.

Rosa didn't move. He got up and stormed toward her. Rosa knew the drivers carried guns, so she was relieved not

to see one in his hand. Then he grabbed her coat sleeve. She knew better than to confront this kind of man.

"I will get off," Rosa answered in her soft-spoken way. She mustered the courage to add, "I know one thing, you better not hit me."

As Rosa descended the steps, she heard a black passenger in the back mutter, "She ought to get off and go around the back like everyone else." *They're tired,* Rosa thought. *They want to go home, and I'm holding them up.* But they were so afraid of fighting back that it made her angry. She didn't get back on; she just kept walking. And she vowed always to check who was driving before she stepped onto a bus again.

WORKING FOR CHANGE

PROTEST

Raymond inspired Rosa to join the NAACP, too. At her first meeting, she was the only woman there, and she was elected secretary. Too timid to say no, Rosa accepted and began working for Edgar Nixon, answering calls from people with complaints of injustice. Nixon was a bold, no-nonsense crusader for black rights. A railway porter, he had earned his own living since he was fourteen.

Change was brewing in the South. Nixon and Parks excitedly followed news of blacks in Baton Rouge, Louisiana, who were refusing to ride the city's segregated buses to protest the seating laws. Then, in 1954, the United States Supreme Court made a far-reaching decision that thrilled Rosa Parks. "Separate but equal" schooling was a lie, it declared. No one needed to tell Rosa that. She'd seen firsthand the difference between her crowded, one-room school in Pine Level, where students had to bring their own kindling to heat the place, and the big new brick school where the white children went. But soon segregated schools would be illegal across the country! Rosa felt she was stepping into a new, hopeful time.

BROWN V. BOARD OF EDUCATION OF TOPEKA "SEPARATE BUT EQUAL" STRUCK DOWN

In the early 1950s, the NAACP filed class-action suits on behalf of black students denied entrance to white schools. In 1954, the Supreme Court ruled unanimously that racial segregation in public schools violated the Fourteenth Amendment to the Constitution, which guaranteed equal protection under the law to everyone. The decision rejected the "separate but equal" argument that had been used since 1896. The judges declared that forcing a group to attend separate schools created a sense of inferiority and denied them opportunities.

Local school authorities and district courts were ordered to integrate schools "with all deliberate speed." Yet many southern public schools were slow to obey, refusing integration until the late 1960s.

Following the court order to integrate schools, six-year-old Ruby Bridges is escorted under the protection of U.S. Deputy Marshals to and from elementary school in New Orleans, despite the resistance of many white parents.

The bus boycott in Baton Rouge ended when its leader accepted a weak compromise. Edgar Nixon felt the protesters had been tricked and let down, but it had been so promising. He and the other NAACP leaders started talking. Why not try it in Montgomery? Some thirty thousand blacks rode the city's **MASS BOYCOTT** buses, far outnumbering white passengers. A mass boycott would cost the bus company a lot of money and force it to change its rules. In fact, Nixon wanted to go even further: he wanted to challenge the segregation laws themselves. If someone were arrested and charged for violating the segregation law, an appeal could be launched that could go all the way to the Supreme Court.

What Nixon and the NAACP needed was the perfect plaintiff. Someone law-abiding and honest, someone the white newspapers and politicians wouldn't be able to call a criminal and troublemaker. A woman would be best, Nixon reasoned; she'd get more sympathy than a black man. Her life would have to be spotless: no crimes or embarrassing brushes with the law. A couple of people had already been arrested for refusing to give up their bus seat, but they'd had troubled pasts or had fought with the driver. Nixon would have to wait until the right person came along.

THE CRUCIAL MOMENT

On December 1, 1955, Rosa Parks worked her usual long day in the basement tailor shop at the Montgomery Fair department store. It was hot among the huge steam presses, and employees had to smile and be polite no matter how rude the customers were. At 5:00 p.m. she left work and walked a block to wait for her usual bus. The streets were crowded with Christmas shoppers; the bus lines were long. As she boarded the bus, her mind was filled with all the tasks she had to do for the NAACP. She saw an empty aisle seat in the middle section, where blacks or whites could sit, depending on the driver's rules. The three passengers already sitting in that row were black, so she took the empty seat.

At the next two stops more white passengers boarded and filled the front. One man was left standing.

The driver turned around. "Let me have those front seats," he said.

Parks glanced up and her heart sank. It was the same driver who'd forced her off his bus a dozen years earlier. She'd been too distracted to notice him when she boarded. She understood what he wanted. She and the three other people in her row would have to move to the back and stand. A white man wanted to sit, and he mustn't have a black person next to him. There was silence throughout the bus, and for a moment no one moved.

"Y'all better make it light on yourselves and let me have those seats," the driver shouted this time, his red face set in an ugly scowl.

The two women across the aisle from Parks suddenly rose at the same time and quietly walked to the back. The man next to Rosa stood up, and she twisted in her seat to let him pass. Then Rosa did something no one expected. She slid along the bench to the window and sat looking outside.

How is standing up going to "make it light" for me? she thought. *The more we give in, the worse they treat us.* She could hear the driver get up and walk toward her, but she kept her eyes on the window.

The driver stopped, towering above her. "You gonna stand up?" he demanded.

Rosa's single-word reply was clearly heard through the silent bus: "No."

"Well, I'm going to have you arrested."

"You may do that," Rosa said softly.

The driver spun on his heel and walked to the front of the bus to radio his supervisor. It was clear to Rosa he had no memory of ever seeing her before. *Why would he? I'm just another black woman.* In fact, the driver seemed perplexed by this prim, tidy woman in her sensible coat and wire-rimmed glasses, openly defying him.

She watched him call his supervisor on the radio, then get off the bus and stand waiting on the sidewalk. *He must have called the police,* Rosa thought. *He's waiting for them.*

She knew that black people who broke the law could be beaten by the police. *Better not to imagine what is going to happen next,* she told herself. She might lose her nerve. Around her, passengers, black and white, started to get off the bus, no one speaking above a whisper. *Wouldn't it be wonderful,* she thought, *if the other three had also refused to move?* Or if everyone in the back had stuck together? But no, it was just her now. She'd made her choice and the others had made theirs; she wouldn't blame them for that.

UNDER ARREST

Two policemen arrived and climbed into the bus. One of them asked Rosa why she didn't get up.

"Why do you all push us around?" she answered, surprised at her own boldness.

The officer was tongue-tied for an instant. "I—I don't know," he stammered, "but the law is the law, and you're under arrest."

The officers picked up her purse and shopping bag and escorted her off the bus. No one touched her as they led her to the police car, handing her bags in after she was seated in the back.

At the city jail, Parks was surprised at how unafraid she was. She felt resigned, ready to face whatever came. She asked for a drink of water and to make a phone call. No, they said to both. For the first time she felt angry, but she didn't let it show.

She emptied her purse and pockets, was fingerprinted and photographed, then taken to a cell. At last a guard took her to make a phone call. The guard dialed her home, and Rosa told her mother and husband where she was. "No, they didn't beat me," she reassured her anxious mother, and she asked Raymond to hurry to come get her.

Police photo of Rosa Parks, taken at the time of her arrest

Some passengers on the bus had recognized Rosa Parks and gotten in touch with Nixon. Shocked, he quickly called one of Montgomery's two black lawyers, but couldn't reach him. With no time to lose, he contacted a white lawyer, Clifford Durr. Durr often championed black rights, and his wife was friendly with Rosa. He called the jail and was dismayed to learn that Rosa Parks was being charged with violating the city's segregation laws. Nixon rushed there to post her bail.

Flanked by guards, Rosa walked through the iron mesh doors and saw the Durrs and Nixon waiting for her. Raymond, driven by a friend, raced to the front of the jail moments later, and gave Rosa a bear hug. Rosa was suddenly too overwhelmed to speak. The arrest had upset her more than she'd realized. Around her the others talked angrily. "This must never happen again!" they said, outraged. All Rosa could think was, *I am never getting on a segregated bus again in my life, even if I have to walk to work until the end of my days.*

"THE PERFECT PLAINTIFF"

Nixon and the others stayed at the Parks home until late that night, when Nixon took Parks aside. This, he told her, could be the very test case against segregation they had been waiting for. "Will *you* be our plaintiff?" he asked.

Strangely, she hadn't thought of that possibility until this moment. She'd never been a fighter on the front lines; she'd always worked quietly behind the scenes. Could she be the perfect plaintiff they'd hoped for? Nixon said yes—no police record, she'd worked hard all her life, and everyone who knew her was amazed at how she seemed to have no temper, never a mean word to say about anyone. Nothing but being born black had caused her arrest.

Parks hesitated. She weighed the risks in her mind. She'd be an outcast in Montgomery—she already expected to be fired because of her arrest, but if she persisted, what white business would ever hire her? Raymond might be arrested on some phony charge. Her frail mother might not be able to stand the ordeal of a trial. "I'll have to talk it over with Raymond," she said.

Raymond was upset. "It could go wrong, Rosa, you could get hurt!" But slowly he changed his mind. Rosa felt her fears fade, too. Yes, she finally told Nixon. Before midnight it was decided: black attorney Fred Gray would be Parks's lawyer. She would plead not guilty and challenge the segregation laws.

BOLD PLANS

Rosa's trial would be on Monday. It was Thursday night, and everyone knew there was much to do. Word of the arrest was spread among Montgomery's black activists. Fred Gray called teacher Jo Ann Robinson, head of the Women's Political Council, a group dedicated to ending segregation. On hearing the news, Robinson immediately declared that they needed a Monday boycott of the buses to protest Rosa's trial. She and her students worked through the night to copy thousands of handbills. Students would hand them out in all the black schools in the morning, telling children to take them home to their parents. Others would take them to homes and churches.

Nixon was thrilled by Robinson's bold plan. At 5:00 a.m. he called the city's black ministers—they could convince thousands to stay off the buses on Monday if they preached about the boycott on Sunday. A friend suggested he also call a new young minister, Martin Luther King Jr. They agreed to an emergency meeting that night at King's church.

BOYCOTT THE BUSES

Nixon had to hurry to catch his train for his porter job, but he arranged a last-minute meeting on the station platform with a sympathetic reporter. He gave the reporter the handbill, hoping the newspaper would print the story.

Friday evening, Rosa Parks hurried to Dexter Avenue Baptist Church to hear the ministers. She was glad to learn that King had joined the cause. She'd heard him preach and was impressed by the straightforward passion of his words. When Parks slipped into the church basement, the scene was not promising. Fifty leaders were arguing, by no means united in supporting a boycott. A few people looked imploringly at her. As she stood up, a hush fell. She told the story of her arrest, and said simply that collective action was needed now. Many ministers shifted in their seats, embarrassed. Who wanted to look like someone who abandoned a good woman in her time of crisis? In the end, most ministers agreed to tell parishioners about the Monday boycott.

Dexter Avenue Baptist Church, where Martin Luther King Jr. was pastor

They rewrote the handbill, adding, "Come to a mass meeting Monday at 7:00 p.m. at the Holt Street Baptist Church, for further instruction."

On Sunday morning Parks was thrilled to see the handbill on the front page of the *Montgomery Advertiser*. A good sign! The black-owned taxi companies had even promised to charge boycotters just ten cents for a ride, the same as bus fare. But would enough people stay off the buses? She thought of all those who'd slipped away silently when she had refused to move. Would it be the same tomorrow?

SISTER ROSA!

Or what if they did stay off, but were attacked by angry whites? If people were hurt or killed, she'd never forgive herself.

THE BOYCOTT BEGINS

Monday morning the sky was dark and threatened rain. Rosa's mother called her to the window. "Come quickly, look!" she said, parting the curtain. Rosa ran to her side. The 6:00 a.m. rush-hour bus was roaring past her building. It was nearly empty, without a single black rider. So were the others that came after. Her eyes brimmed with tears at the sight of one empty bus after another.

Parks dressed neatly in a plain black dress and gray coat and headed to the courthouse with Raymond for her trial. On the way they passed streets full of black workers walking, and saw more empty buses.

As Rosa and Raymond approached the steps of City Hall, hundreds of people were waiting for them. Supporters burst into applause. At the foot of the stairs the NAACP youth group shouted, "Sister Rosa!" That's when one of the girls cried out, "Oh, she's so sweet—they've messed with the wrong one now!"

Rosa Parks entered the courtroom, Fred Gray and Mont-gomery's other black lawyer, Charles Langford, on either side of her. *There's nothing to fear*, she told herself. All she had to do was wait for her moment to say, "Not guilty." When her eyes met those of the scowling driver, she felt only pity. *So full of hatred*, she thought.

The trial lasted five minutes. Fred Gray argued that segregation was a violation of a citizen's constitutional rights, but the judge was unimpressed and Rosa Parks was convicted. She was fined ten dollars plus court costs.

A NEW LEADER

That night she headed to the rally at Holt Street Baptist Church. They'd chosen a location in a poor, black neighbor-hood—the kind of place the city's whites avoided—so black citizens wouldn't be afraid to attend. As she hurried down the dark streets she was amazed by what she saw. Thousands of people had turned out, filling streets for blocks around the church. Cars were halted in traffic jams. As she got nearer she saw loudspeakers had been set up to address the crowd out-side. A thousand people had squeezed into the church, but many more thronged outside.

Parks squirmed through the crowd. Inside, Nixon was already standing up to speak. One question was on everyone's mind: Was the boycott over, or should it go on? Rosa knew many people were afraid of going too far. They'd been successful today, but it wouldn't be long before Montgomery's whites got angry. "Even if it goes on, there's no way it'll last longer than a week," people around her murmured. *They're probably right,* she thought.

Nixon's speech made it clear which side he was on. "You who are afraid," he announced, "you'd better get your hat and coat and go home. This is going to be a long drawn-out affair." Then he handed over the meeting to the new minister, Martin Luther King Jr. Earlier that day, they had founded a new organization to run the boycott, the Montgomery Improvement Association (MIA). King was elected its leader.

King's voice filled the air: "Since it had to happen, I'm happy it happened to a person like Rosa Parks, for nobody can doubt the boundless outreach of her integrity. Nobody can doubt the height of her character, nobody can doubt the depth of her Christian commitment." Each piece of praise was met with loud applause, to Rosa's growing embarrassment.

When the crowd had hushed he went on.

"There comes a time when people get tired. We are here this evening to say to those who have mistreated us so long that we are tired—tired of being segregated and humiliated;  tired of being kicked about by the brutal feet of oppression … For many years we have shown amazing patience. We have sometimes given our white brothers the feeling that we liked the way we were being treated. But we come here tonight to be saved from that patience that makes us patient with anything less than freedom and justice."

Martin Luther King Jr.
during a civil rights march

His words thrilled the tightly packed crowd in the church. Booming on the loudspeakers outside, his voice was met with cheers and people shouting "Amen!" in the streets. King hugged Rosa Parks and introduced her to the crowd, who began to chant her name. Seeing her shyness, he quietly told her that she didn't need to speak; her actions had already spoken for her. Parks nodded, relieved. It was enough just to be there, to be a part of it.

Another minister read the list of demands the MIA would show the bus company and the city's politicians. The boycott would end on three conditions: courteous treatment of all passengers, black and white; first-come seating with whites in front and blacks in back—no passengers should be required to give up their seats; and the hiring of black drivers for bus routes in black neighborhoods. He asked the crowd if they wanted to carry on the boycott and make those demands, and to stand if their vote was yes. After a pause, a couple of people got to their feet here and there. Then more rose, until the whole church was standing. Standing, too, Rosa Parks could hear the din of the crowd outside, chanting, "Yes!"

BATTLE OF WILLS

Nixon was right: the boycotters were in for a long fight. At King and Gray's first meeting with the bus company and city authorities, their demands were flatly refused. The boycotters faced a big challenge: thirty thousand people had to get to and from work each day without the bus. Most did not have cars. The MIA scrambled to make it possible. Parks helped organize a complex system of carpools. Black-owned taxis continued to pick up passengers at the bus stops, charging them ten cents. Many walked until their shoes wore out.

White city authorities fought back. There could be no compromise—if you gave an inch, they believed, the black community would demand a mile. Instead they tried to undermine the boycott. Intimidation would be their chief weapon.

Police harassed people waiting on corners for their carpool or taxi. They threatened to arrest taxi drivers who didn't

People Who Said No

charge full fare. Whites who gave their black employees a lift to work were bombarded with hate mail.

The city's black churches bought station wagons to help with the carpool. "Rolling churches," whites sneered. Police started pulling over the station wagons, arresting drivers for breaking the slightest traffic law. The mayor even tried to get a court order declaring the riders waiting on corners a "public nuisance." Racist groups such as the White Citizens' Council and the Ku Klux Klan swelled with new members who were alarmed at the show of pride among the city's blacks.

PUT TO THE TEST

Rosa didn't have to worry long about how she would get to work. Her boss told her the tailor shop was closing. He wasn't firing her because of her arrest, but still she was out of work. She took in sewing jobs at home.

A week later, Raymond came home with bad news. He'd quit his job at the barbershop when his boss had forbidden anyone to talk about Rosa Parks or the bus boycott. "How can I work in a place where my wife's name is forbidden?" he asked Rosa, who couldn't blame him. Christmas came and went, and the new year began with Rosa and Raymond struggling to pay the rent. Rosa started to worry about Raymond, who often answered their phone only to hear death threats against her.

But Parks was heartened to see that her early faith in King was justified. Her admiration grew as he made it clear he would never resort to violence to gain their victory. "Our weapons are protest and love," he often said.

OUR WEAPONS ARE PROTEST AND LOVE

That commitment was tested on January 30. King was speaking to the regular Monday night meeting of boycotters.

A breathless friend rushed in, saying a bomb had gone off in King's house. King knew his wife and young daughter were there. Staying calm, he reassured everyone and hurried home. A crowd was gathered already, including the nervous police commissioner and mayor, who feared a riot. The front window was blown apart and the porch had sunk into a crater, but King's wife and baby were unhurt. Outside, he spoke to the angry onlookers, urging them to forget revenge. Even if he were killed, he said, others would carry on the fight for equal rights.

In February the city tried a new tactic. They revived an old, ignored state law from 1921 that forbade boycotts in Alabama. A grand jury indicted Rosa Parks and eighty-eight others, including Martin Luther King Jr. Instead of waiting at home to be arrested, Parks walked to the courthouse and asked for the sheriff.

EQUAL RIGHTS

"Are you looking for me?" she asked calmly. "Well, I am here."

In March, King was the only one to be convicted, and he was cheered by crowds as he left the courthouse. It made him even more of a hero to the anti-segregationists, black and white. Parks traveled the country to speak about the boycott, and the impression she made with her quiet dignity drew new supporters for the cause.

A BREAKTHROUGH FOR EQUALITY

The boycott everyone thought could only last a week dragged on for over a year. Meanwhile, the lawsuit challenging Montgomery's and Alabama's bus segregation laws went all the way to the Supreme Court. The MIA had decided that challenging Rosa Parks's conviction could prove to be a dead end—her case might never get past Alabama's state court. Instead, they filed a federal lawsuit to challenge the constitutionality of bus segregation. On November 13, 1956, the Supreme Court judges announced their decision. Segregation was illegal.

Blacks in Montgomery rejoiced, the streets filled with singing, cheering, and honking car horns as the news spread. The city appealed the decision one last time—and lost. On December 20, the court order was served, and by law, Montgomery's buses were fully integrated. In triumph, King and the other boycott leaders boarded the first integrated bus, sitting side by side with the few whites who had supported them.

Rosa Parks stayed home that day to take care of her mother. Answering a knock at the door, she was greeted by three bashful reporters. Could she come ride a bus today, they asked, so they could take pictures of the historic event? It seemed silly to Parks to stage such a display, but they convinced her at last. Boarding a neighborhood bus, Rosa was stunned for a moment to see who was driving—James Blake, the driver who had called for her arrest. There was only one thing to do. She ignored him as she passed, and he did the

Rosa Parks poses for reporters on the day Montgomery's buses were integrated by law.

same to her. The reporters had no idea who he was. They asked her to sit down and gaze out the window, just as she had on December 1, 1955.

After a few violent acts of revenge against the boycotters—snipers shot at King's house, another minister's home was bombed—the city's integrated buses began running smoothly. And the success of Montgomery's boycotters inspired a wave of other protests. Across the country, black and white students staged sit-ins at segregated lunch counters, and organized "freedom rides" on the interstate buses to demand an end to segregation everywhere.

STRUGGLE

Despite the victory, Rosa Parks's life in Montgomery was troubled. The death threats continued, and it was hard for her and Raymond to find jobs. Racism did not disappear from the city overnight. Rosa and Raymond decided to move to Detroit, where her brother Sylvester lived. There she continued the struggle for equality, working for a progressive politician, taking part in protest marches, and speaking in schools about civil rights. In 1963, she joined the massive March on Washington for Jobs and Freedom with Martin Luther King Jr.

In 1964, largely thanks to King and those who struggled alongside him, the Civil Rights Act was passed in Congress. It guaranteed equal rights for all races in the United States. King won the Nobel Peace Prize the same year.

People called Rosa Parks the mother of the Montgomery bus boycott, and later the mother of the civil rights movement. She knew she had become a symbol and always tried to tell her story simply and honestly. People would describe her as a "tired seamstress," too weary to give up her seat, and this story spread, eclipsing what had really happened.

Rosa would shake her head. "The only tired I was," she would say, "was tired of giving in."

THE NOBEL PEACE PRIZE

The six Nobel Prizes are the legacy of Alfred Nobel, a wealthy Swedish industrialist. When he died in 1896, his will established a fund to reward, each year, extraordinary work by scientists, doctors, writers, and those who promote peace. The yearly peace award ceremony takes place in Oslo, Norway. Famous winners include Mother Teresa, Andrei Sakharov, and Desmond Tutu.

Mother Teresa, a nun who devoted herself to helping the poorest people in India, won the Nobel Peace Prize in 1979. She founded the Missionaries of Charity, who care for the poor in many countries.

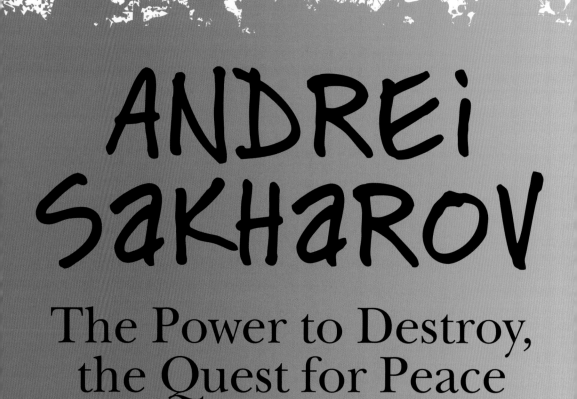

ANDREi SaKHaROV

The Power to Destroy, the Quest for Peace

Soviet Union, 1953

The flash was almost blinding, then a huge white ball lit up the vast horizon. On impulse, Andrei Sakharov ripped off his dark goggles to see better. He peered through the glare at the massive gray cloud that rose, streaming purple, then glinting with orange. Soon it looked like the mushroom shape he'd seen in pictures. They had done it.

"The savior of Russia!"

A powerful hand slapped him on the back, and Andrei turned to look into the face of a grinning general. His genius would be rewarded. He was about to be showered with honors, made one of the Soviet Union's elite, enjoying a life of privilege.

No pangs of conscience about his lethal creation troubled him, not yet. He was a patriot, a soldier in the new scientific war. Perhaps the slightest unease brooded in the back of his mind, and for now, he pushed it away. Yet very soon those misgivings would awaken ideas that he would not be able to ignore, and push him toward a choice that would put everything at risk: his honors, his privileges, even his freedom.

YOUNG DREAMER

Fifteen years earlier, in 1938, a tall, lanky boy with a mop of dark hair shuffled into his first class at Moscow University. No one noticed him as he sat in the back, but Andrei was used to feeling invisible. Maybe it was all those years his parents had homeschooled him, sheltering him from the troubled world of the new communist Russia. His own dreamy nature tuned out the rest. Now, at seventeen, he still hadn't discovered how to break out of his shell and make friends.

THE SOVIET UNION IS BORN

In 1917, a people's revolution overthrew the czars who ruled Russia and founded a new society based on the ideas of Karl Marx. The new order was known as communism: a society without social classes, in which all property was shared and people were paid according to their needs. Russia and other neighboring republics were now ruled by *soviets*, revolutionary councils of workers. These republics joined together, and the new state was named the Union of Soviet Socialist Republics (USSR), also known as the Soviet Union.

While Marx predicted that government would wither away once the workers had risen up and destroyed the capitalist system, no such thing happened in the Soviet Union. The state, run by the Communist Party, grew in size and power, controlling every aspect of people's lives. And the new Communist government did not feel secure, so one of their chief aims was to destroy resistance from those who would "turn back the clock" and undo the revolution.

By the 1930s, when Andrei Sakharov was a teenager, the Soviet Union had plunged into frightening times. Millions were starving as Russia's vast farmlands were turned into government-owned collectives. Joseph Stalin, the new leader of the Communist Party, was the most ruthless yet in rooting out opponents. People denounced one another to avoid being next. Stalin targeted entire classes of people as enemies of the state, and millions perished.

This government photo shows happy farmworkers. In reality, life on the new Communist collectives was much grimmer.

As class began, Andrei hung back shyly while the others debated. He didn't take notes; he knew he'd remember it all. He was here because he had recently discovered something that changed his life. He had always found math ridiculously easy, but he had never found anything that could completely fascinate him—until he opened a book on physics, the key to all matter and energy. He was hooked. Here was a whole world beyond the problems of any one little person. Here were miracles he could understand.

In the physics club, he even forgot his shyness. Andrei would jump from one idea to another, arriving at a solution in a flash, without bothering to explain all the steps in between. Others were amazed to see the skinny boy scribbling on the blackboard with his left or right hand—both were just as fast—solving puzzles in minutes that might take them a whole day.

As for the required classes in Marxism, he yawned through those—not that he questioned any of it. But in science, truth was international, so politics bored him.

Through it all, Andrei carried with him a secret wish, something to make his lone life worthwhile. To uncover the secrets of nature—*that* would make him happy.

WAR AND A CHANGED WORLD

In 1941, the country plunged into crisis, carrying Andrei along with it. At the beginning of World War II, Germany and the Soviet Union had signed a secret nonaggression pact: they would stay neutral to each other, and would divide the countries of Eastern Europe between them. But Germany broke its pact with the Soviet Union and invaded. Over 4 million soldiers cut a brutal path for the capital, Moscow. After the initial shock, everyone scrambled to help ward off the invasion.

Andrei reported to the air force for the medical exam to ensure he was fit for duty. They told him he had an incurable heart condition. He would not be fighting.

Everything happened faster in wartime—university programs were squeezed into fewer years, and Andrei soon graduated with a degree in defense metallurgy. His teacher encouraged him to keep studying "pure science," but Andrei felt strongly that, as a scientist, he should do something practical for the war effort.

He was assigned to a weapons factory south of Moscow, where he was presented with a challenge: find a way to test armor-piercing shells. This was an urgent task. The German assault depended upon its tanks, and Soviet soldiers were fending them off with batches of dud shells that were costing them their lives. Sakharov solved the problem simply and ingeniously: magnets could quickly sort the good from bad. It was the first time he'd applied science to the real world! His confidence soared.

At the factory he met Klavdia Vikhireva, one of the women workers assembling weapons. Klava, as she was called, was Andrei's opposite. Strong and hearty, she liked to swim the Volga River. She was the daughter of peasants, the first of her family to go to university, taking advantage of the Communists' offer of free education for everyone. Klava nursed Andrei to health when he got sick. He asked her to marry him in a letter, a gesture so old-fashioned Klava felt as if she were in a novel.

VICTORY FOR RUSSIA

The war with Germany ended in victory for Russia and its allies, but the country was devastated. A mistrustful Soviet government now cut its citizens off from the West. As British prime minister Winston Churchill declared, it was as if an "iron curtain" had fallen between the Soviet Union and its Western allies.

Andrei and Klava moved to Moscow, where he was eager to return to pure science at the Physics Institute. Apartments were scarce, and they lived in basement rooms, only to be driven out when it suited the landlord. Their room was often so cold, Andrei worked at his desk in a coat.

But Andrei was so preoccupied with science that he barely noticed the world around him. On his way to the bakery one morning, a chance look at a newspaper headline jolted him out of his dream world. The United States had dropped an atom bomb on Hiroshima, Japan. Andrei's legs nearly gave way. In that instant, he felt his fate, and that of the whole world, change. Science had brought something new and incredibly powerful into the world.

A nuclear explosion creates a huge mushroom-shaped cloud of dust and debris.

THE NUCLEAR AGE BEGINS

In 1945, the United States dropped its first atom bomb, alerting the world that it had nuclear weapons, and that warfare had been taken to a new, terrifying level. A single nuclear weapon could be more destructive than all the bombs dropped in World War II combined.

Soviet leader Joseph Stalin was intimidated by such power in the hands of a nation opposed to communism. To survive, he insisted, the Soviet Union must also be a nuclear power. Stalin's regime made catching up with the British and Americans—and surpassing them—a priority. The best scientists were recruited, while hundreds of thousands of prisoners were forced to labor in mining and construction. Secrecy was crucial. The enemy must not be able to steal Soviet designs, and must always be kept guessing as to how much power the USSR wielded.

The race for nuclear superiority and the hostility between the United States and the Soviet Union became known as the Cold War, and it lasted until roughly 1990, creating a climate of fear around the world. Global destruction seemed to be a constant threat, and the two nuclear powers came to the brink of war more than once, most dangerously in 1962, in a showdown over Soviet nuclear weapons in Cuba.

The number of nuclear weapons built by the U.S. and the Soviet Union reached a peak at around 32,000 each. Thousands have been dismantled since the end of the Cold War.

Soviet missiles from the Cold War era, positioned for launch

ORDERS FROM THE TOP

"We've been following your progress for quite a while," the husky man in uniform said, his voice a reassuring purr. It didn't match the rest of him, intimidating in his general's uniform. Andrei Sakharov squirmed. He had received a mysterious invitation to a meeting at this Moscow hotel. Now he stood awkwardly, looking about a room that was more like an office. He glanced up at the huge portrait of Stalin on the wall, then back down at the desk below it and met the eyes of General Zverev.

"We'd like you to work with us on state projects of the greatest importance. You'll have the best of everything— libraries, equipment, the best pay and living conditions. We know you have a housing problem; you'll be given an apartment in Moscow, even if you're assigned elsewhere for a while."

Joseph Stalin, the Communist leader who dominated the Soviet Union from 1922 to 1953

Assigned elsewhere? Sakharov coughed nervously, glancing at the portrait again, which seemed to scowl down at him. *We,* Sakharov thought. *He keeps saying that. Who is "we"?* But he didn't ask, and the general didn't tell him. The housing promise was tempting.

Sakharov swallowed and said no, thank you. At the Institute he was doing what he loved, and he couldn't abandon it.

"I hope you'll reconsider," the general said quietly.

One evening, Sakharov's superior at the Institute, Igor Tamm, called Sakharov and another student into his office. Their teacher's behavior was strangely secretive.

"I've received orders," Tamm said, adding in a whisper, "from the very top." Sakharov and his fellow student glanced at each other. "I'm to lead a team with a special task"—Tamm paused—"to explore the possibilities of building a thermonuclear weapon."

The words were still sinking in when Tamm added, "I've been told to take my best students." That meant Andrei. This time it was not an offer, but an order.

THE CHALLENGE OF A LIFETIME

Andrei Sakharov was about to be ushered into a world of secrets. Even the names of everything connected to the project were meant to hide what lay behind them. The "Ministry of Medium Machine Building" was engaged in building a "device"; the laboratory, far from Moscow, where weapons were developed, was called the "Installation." In early 1949, Sakharov was told he was being transferred from Tamm's team to work at the Installation.

He was escorted into the ministry's private train car, surrounded by men in uniform and plainclothes agents. The train was taking him to Sarov, a town that no longer appeared on any Soviet maps. Fidgeting in his seat, Andrei couldn't

WHAT IS A NUCLEAR WEAPON?

A nuclear weapon is a bomb that gets its force from *nuclear fission*, *nuclear fusion*, or both.

Atomic bombs use fission. Energy is released when the nucleus (the central core) of a uranium or plutonium atom is split.

Thermonuclear bombs, or hydrogen bombs, use fusion. In fusion bombs, nuclei are forced together under extremely high temperatures. Thermonuclear bombs can be thousands of times more powerful than atomic bombs.

Nuclear bombs or warheads are the most destructive explosive weapons ever made. They produce a powerful blast spreading outward from the point of detonation, known as a *shock wave*. They also generate intense light that can blind, heat that causes fires, and deadly *fallout*—radioactive particles that fall to Earth. Some particles land later, far from the site of the explosion. Fallout is hazardous to human and animal life.

An early Soviet nuclear bomb

escape a feeling of foreboding. Yet his nervousness was mixed with excitement, and deep inside he was flattered by all the security and fuss. His work would be truly important! That thought helped. The train sped through the night, but Andrei couldn't sleep.

At dawn he was in Sarov, and being taken by car past peasant huts and cows to a complex surrounded by barbed wire. Nothing gave a clue to the purpose of the huge hexagonal complex. The local peasants believed that an ideal communist community was being tested inside.

Within the buildings, Sakharov was relieved to see a familiar face, a scientist named Yakov Zeldovich. Stocky and bald, Zeldovich was a fireball of energy, and his excitement about any scientific project was contagious. Sakharov felt more at ease. Zeldovich introduced him to the other scientists, and Sakharov reddened as they stared at him, surveying his shabby suit. But he quickly started to feel at home. Everyone was hardworking, laboring around the clock when needed.

Soon Andrei's wife and children were moving into a large apartment in Moscow. But it would be a while before they could join Andrei. The KGB, the state secret police, were running a security check of Klava. In the meantime, there would be no letters or phone calls between Andrei and his family. He turned twenty-nine, far from his wife and daughters.

The team at the Installation was given five years to create a thermonuclear bomb. Andrei was fueled by excitement over the challenge. He had found a scientist's paradise. "A thermonuclear reaction—the mysterious source of the energy of sun and stars, the sustenance of life on Earth but also the potential instrument of its destruction—was within my grasp, taking place right on my desk!" he wrote. Any misgivings he'd had about creating weapons vanished. Most important, he

told himself, his work was essential to his country. In his heart he believed what his government told him: the world war had ended, but the Soviet Union was still at war with enemies who wanted to destroy it. Andrei felt like a soldier in this new scientific war. The bomb he was helping to create would, he was sure, deter attacks against his country. Only if the Soviets were as strong as their enemies could there be peace.

The other scientists at the Installation soon got to know Andrei's odd ways. He'd arrive wearing shoes that didn't match, and didn't care when it was pointed out to him. The security guards were taught to recognize Sakharov on sight. He would walk into work completely distracted, his mind absorbed in solving a problem, and instead of his security pass, he would fish out a scribbled formula and wave it at the guard.

At last Klava passed her background check, and she and their two daughters came to live with Andrei in a house at the Installation. But Andrei had sunk deeper into what he called a "strange and fantastic" world. Each evening, returning to ordinary family life was a shock. His daughters were baffled when he broke off in the middle of a bedtime story, staring ahead, his mind far away.

A CRITICAL TEST

They had been given five years to create the bomb; the device was ready to be tested ahead of schedule, in four. Much had happened in the meantime. Stalin had died, and Nikita Khrushchev was now leader of the Soviet Union. Toiling at the Installation, Sakharov had barely noticed the dramatic events of the Cold War. He had made the critical breakthrough, the "First Idea," as he called it: a sphere made of concentric circles, each layer magnifying the reaction within it. The scientists nicknamed it the "Layer Cake." Now, in August 1953, he traveled by train to the test site in remote Kazakhstan—he'd been declared too valuable to fly. The nuclear program was now under the direction of the KGB, and the scientists had a saying: "Medals for success, bullets for failure."

When Sakharov arrived, an uproar was taking place. In their hurry, something vital had been forgotten: fallout—the radioactive particles the explosion would send into the atmosphere. Everyone scrambled to estimate how much radiation the test would produce, flipping hurriedly through a stolen

RADIATION American manual on nuclear explosions. They faced two choices. They could drop the bomb from an airplane rather than from a tower. This could mean a six-month delay. Or they could evacuate tens of thousands of people who lived downwind, but it was estimated that thirty people could be killed in the rush. Orders from the top were clear: remove the people, test on schedule.

Now, in the observation tower, thirty-two kilometers (twenty miles) from ground zero, Sakharov waited. The countdown began. He and the others put on the dark goggles that would shield their eyes. He stood frozen, staring across the grassy steppe as the last seconds were counted. Soon he would know if his idea worked or not.

A brilliant flash, then the horizon was glowing, the white ball turning gray and rising. His safety goggles torn away, he drank in every detail with his eyes.

Then a shock wave blasted his ears and knocked him backward. As he staggered up, his ears filled with a long rumble that slowly died away. The cloud filled half the sky now, turning blue-black.

Elated, Sakharov and a handful of team members drove toward ground zero to get a closer look. As soon as the jeep halted, Sakharov jumped out and walked toward what was left of the tower from which the bomb had dropped. The once-grassy ground was now a black crust that splintered under his feet like glass.

The "device" was a complete success. Andrei Sakharov was the hero of the hour. He was unanimously elected to the Soviet Academy of Sciences, an honor that took some people twenty years to achieve. He was invited to the Kremlin and pinned with medals: Hero of Socialist Labor, the highest civilian honor, and the Stalin Prize.

Then, in November, he started having nosebleeds and

The Kremlin, a citadel that houses the government in Moscow

came down with a fever. He said nothing, but wondered, *Was it the radiation at ground zero, where I walked around so carelessly?*

Klava began to hate living at the Installation. She felt snubbed by the intellectuals around her. But worse was the constant surveillance. Andrei shrugged. He knew they were always watched. He'd been assigned two "secretaries," really bodyguards, who followed him everywhere. He ignored them, just as he shut out many realities, but Klava couldn't. She and the children began spending more time in their Moscow apartment, and Andrei was often alone. His one friend remained Zeldovich.

REPERCUSSIONS

Soon they were working on a new "device." Scientist Vitaly Ginzburg had improved on Sakharov's First Idea. But Sakharov and Zeldovich took it further, perfecting it. Fall 1955 was set as the test date, and the scientists worked feverishly to meet it. Sakharov didn't have time to make all the necessary calculations, and he began to rely on intuition. Others noticed his uncanny ability to predict results, as if he could imagine exactly how an electron would behave.

Sakharov and Zeldovich traveled again to the Kazakh steppes to witness the test of their "Third Idea." It would produce a much more powerful blast than before. The vast steppe was covered with light snow. Standing on a platform, Sakharov watched the distant white airplane carrying the bomb soar upward. *Like a predator about to strike*, he thought. This time he didn't wear the dark goggles; he wanted to miss nothing. He turned his back when the voice on the loud-speaker cried, "The bomb has dropped!"

As soon as the horizon before him lit up, he whirled around and was nearly blinded by the white sphere that swelled at an alarming rate. Dust rose, transforming into a swirling gray-blue cloud, flashing crimson. Beneath it, a mush-roomlike stem formed, more massive than in the previous blast. Sakharov's face burned with heat, even though the temperature outside was freezing. No one spoke.

Minutes passed. This time he saw the shock wave coming, flattening down the grass as it raced across the steppe toward them.

"Jump!" he shouted and leaped off the platform. Every-one did the same. Sakharov's ears were blasted, his body hit with a force that knocked the breath from him. Dimly, he heard the sound of breaking glass. He lay dazed. Then Zeldovich was running toward him, shouting, "It worked! It worked!" He pulled Sakharov into a hug.

Hours later, Sakharov heard news that wiped away his smile. The shock wave had claimed two victims: a soldier inside a collapsing trench and a little girl in an old bomb shelter. *It wasn't my fault*, he told himself. *Who could have foreseen it?* But he couldn't shake a terrible feeling. He was responsible.

AN URGENT PLEA

Still somber that night at the banquet, Sakharov stood up, raising his glass for a toast. "May all our devices explode as successfully as today's, but always over test sites and never over cities."

The table of military officers and scientists sat in cold silence. Sakharov stood there, awkward and helpless. At last a sneering marshal rose and barked out a sarcastic joke, as if Sakharov had never spoken. Soon everyone was talking again, too fast, and laughing too loudly. Sakharov sat back down among them, completely ignored. He felt as if he'd been stung by a whip.

As the voices buzzed around him, Andrei saw something for the first time with terrible clarity. He and his comrades had created a weapon, the most powerful in human history. And now they had no control over who would use it, or when.

He threw himself into a new set of calculations. This time he was afraid to predict the results. He needed to know the probable number of deaths from radioactive fallout caused by testing the bombs. Before he even finished, it was clear the number would be staggering. He pushed away the papers, horrified. What had he done?

Sakharov published his findings in a Soviet scientific journal in 1958. He still believed in his own government's good intentions—they just needed to know the danger. "The Soviet state," he wrote, "was compelled to develop nuclear weapons and conduct tests for its security in the face of American and British nuclear weapons." The goal, he insisted, was not destruction but peaceful coexistence, then disarmament, and ultimately the banning of nuclear weapons.

Sakharov contacted Khrushchev himself with a proposal.

AVOID TESTING

There were ways to avoid testing, he explained. Experiments could model the functioning of a bomb without actually dropping it. Khrushchev ignored him. Sakharov was getting a reputation with the authorities. Eccentric but brilliant; he was too high-minded and needed to be put in his place. Sakharov kept pleading against tests—with no success.

He now realized something else. His government had used his brilliance, but he had been a fool to think it wanted his advice. He began to see for the first time how naïve he had been, how blind to consequences!

SPEAKING OUT

In 1964, Khrushchev resigned under pressure from the Communist Party, and Leonid Brezhnev came into power. The new leader was handed reports on the scientist Andrei Sakharov, so valuable and yet so troublesome.

"Sakharov has some doubts and inner conflicts," Brezhnev said. "We ought to try to understand and do all we can to help him." That meant inviting him to join the Communist Party. Sakharov refused, as he always had. But this time the offer had been a test. From now on he was going to be watched even more closely.

Andrei Sakharov

Andrei believed he had nothing to hide. He was a loyal communist, and when he criticized something, it was because he wanted *his* government to be better. At the same time, he was becoming painfully aware of how much he didn't understand about the world. He had toiled away in his scientist's paradise for too long, his head in the sand. He started listening on a shortwave radio to British and American broadcasts, and learned of uprisings against communism in Eastern Europe. Was it possible that his government's misdeeds were even worse than he'd begun to suspect? He started hearing of writers and scientists who'd been sent to labor camps or thrown into psychiatric hospitals for disagreeing with the government.

So many new ideas swirled through his head that he decided to write them down. If only he could fully explain the dangers of the nuclear age! He began work on an article, giving it the title, "Reflections on Progress, Peaceful Coexistence, and Intellectual Freedom." Nuclear weapons, he wrote, had changed the world of humans. War was no longer an option for settling disputes; it was now universal suicide. Anything that divided humankind was therefore a terrible danger,

a "madness and crime." It was a complex problem, and the only way to solve it was through freedom of debate. Dictatorships that stifled freedom of thought were the enemies of the solution that humanity needed to find. Pollution and fallout were global issues, and needed cooperation.

Sakharov handed around a small number of copies. The new head of the KGB, Yuri Andropov, saw the article almost as soon as it was typed. Sakharov had done nothing to hide it—he was constantly spied upon, so what was the point? The new minister of Medium Machine Building was furious, and demanded Sakharov withdraw the document, but Sakharov refused.

The essay was smuggled out of the country, and Sakharov heard on his shortwave radio that it had been published abroad. A copy reached the *New York Times*, where at first the editors doubted that it was genuine. It seemed impossible—a Soviet nuclear physicist arguing against nuclear weapons? But they published it in July 1968. The inner workings of the Soviet Union had long been completely mysterious to people in the West, but now a voice from behind the iron curtain was speaking openly to the world. Within a year, more than 18 million copies were printed worldwide.

UNDER SUSPICION

Andrei Sakharov's life changed. The cover that had hidden his work was now torn away, leaving him not only exposed, but famous. And he faced consequences. He was barred at once from the Installation, sent back to Moscow unemployed. A tragedy followed: Klava died of stomach cancer. In a fit of grief, he gave away all his money to charity. There was only one light in his darkness: an old friend at the Moscow Institute was inviting him to come back to be a pure scientist again.

However, KGB head Andropov had fixed his sights on Sakharov and was not going to let him get away. "Secret listening devices should be installed in Sakharov's apartment," he persuaded the Communist Party's Central Committee, "to give us timely information on Sakharov's intentions and to discover the contacts inciting him to commit hostile acts."

With deadly accuracy, Andropov identified Sakharov's two weaknesses: his scientific pride and his terrible guilt. "Having made a great contribution to the creation of thermonuclear weapons," he declared, "Sakharov felt his 'guilt' before mankind and, because of that, he has set himself the task of fighting for peace."

As for the outrageous article, no mention of it was allowed in Soviet newspapers. Sakharov was not to be named anywhere, even to be criticized. He must not become a spark to ignite anti-government forces. Andropov didn't want to move against him, not yet.

A NEW CAUSE TO FIGHT FOR

Andrei's life took a new direction when he met Elena Bonner, a doctor who made it her mission to help political prisoners. Andrei first saw Elena, talking angrily and dramatically, at the home of a rebellious young scientist. She was as passionate about human rights as he was about science. She was also outspoken and hot-tempered, having once slapped the face of a KGB agent outside a courtroom.

WRITERS AND SCIENTISTS PERSECUTED FOR THEIR BELIEFS

Andrei and Elena married in 1972, at a simple ceremony with two witnesses, and six uninvited KGB agents in dark suits. Andrei was deeply grateful for his new companion. For so long, he realized, he'd set his sights on grand, scientific theories, but now his focus had changed. It was people who mattered—the ones all around him, their rights abused every day. He'd fought against nuclear testing, but from now on his fight must be for human rights.

He used what was left of his great reputation to plead on behalf of writers and scientists persecuted for their beliefs. He cofounded the Committee for Human Rights, a group that would expose the government's abuse of people's freedoms. Sakharov knew he risked disgrace, and worse. He could end up like the very activists he championed—exiled, or locked up in an institution, vanishing from sight. But now that his eyes had been opened, he couldn't just look away. People battling for justice and rebels on the run streamed to Andrei and Elena's apartment for help. Andropov followed it all and reported confidently that Elena Bonner was now the evil influence behind Sakharov's disloyalty.

RECOGNITION, AND GREATER DANGER

Over the next few years, Andrei and Elena made human rights work their mission. One afternoon in 1975, Andrei was drinking tea in a friend's apartment, hiding for a few hours from the constant crowd of people in his own kitchen. A knock on the door shattered his quiet retreat. Two writers stood in the doorway to congratulate him: he had just been awarded the Nobel Peace Prize. Andrei was speechless. He was being honored, they said, not just for his stand against nuclear tests, but for his campaign for peace among countries, and his fight against the abuse of power.

When his excited well-wishers finally left, he realized he faced a dilemma. The government would never let him travel to Norway to accept the prize. But Elena had been allowed to travel abroad for eye surgery. Should he ask her to go for him? Was it putting her in too much danger? He kept changing his mind.

That December, Andrei held his radio to his ear, listening to the sound of Elena's footsteps, then her low voice through the static. Far away in Oslo, she was delivering the speech he had written, accepting the Nobel Prize on his behalf: "Peace, progress, human rights, these three goals are indissolubly linked; it is impossible to achieve one of them if the others are ignored." He listened as she read the long list of every "prisoner of conscience" he knew of in his country. Now their names were being heard by millions.

CAMPAIGN FOR PEACE

"Public Enemy Number One," Andropov called Sakharov, as he slammed his fist on the desk before his fellow KGB agents. But what to do with him? He could never leave the country. He knew too much about the weapons program. But he must not be killed and then revered as a martyr. What remained was Andropov's favorite solution: exile him *within* Russia.

As for Sakharov, he no longer feared for himself—he was resigned to carrying on until the moment he was silenced. But he agonized about his children's safety. What if they were hurt, as a means of punishing him? Still, he felt it was his duty to protest to foreign reporters when the Soviet Union invaded Afghanistan in 1979.

THE EXILE

On a cold January day, Sakharov's car was pulled over by a traffic officer. The back doors opened, and he turned around to glimpse two men climbing in. *It's happening*, he realized. *I'm under arrest.*

All Sakharov's honors were stripped away; he was to be taken immediately to his place of exile. Elena Bonner could go with him if she chose. She was free to go where she liked. The risk was that she wouldn't be allowed to return to Andrei if she left him.

Soon they were huddled together in a van with covered windows, surrounded by KGB agents. They had no way of knowing where they were being taken. But at least they were together.

"Where are we going?" Elena asked, unable to stand the suspense.

"Home," one agent replied with a grin.

Gorky was the name of the city. It wasn't as far away as the labor camps of Siberia, but it was a military city closed to all foreigners. "Mild, by Soviet standards," Andrei muttered to Elena. "A gilded cage." She squeezed his arm.

They were taken to a sparse ground-floor apartment. A police officer would stand guard at their door day and night. Sakharov looked out the dirty front window. Directly across the street, a police station's windows faced his. He glanced around the room; there was no phone. He could go for a walk, but he would be followed, and any more than a few words to a local would be sharply cut off. He did feel like a bird in a cage. He had just been starting to love being with people, and now he would be more isolated than ever.

His spirits rose when Elena opened her suitcase and showed him a shortwave radio she had smuggled. Later she took it on a walk in the nearby woods, and found she could hear news of Andrei's case.

"Why don't you write your memoirs?" Elena suggested in the failing winter light. "You'll have plenty of time," she added dryly. "I'll type." That helped fill the long winter nights. They cooked, talked, and read. Whenever they wanted to say anything private to each other, they wrote notes.

He wrote to his faraway children, now grown up. "How do we live? Tragically. Buried alive. And at the same time, strange as it may seem, happy." It was odd, but true. As long as they were together, it was still possible to feel happy.

CALL FROM MOSCOW

Nearly seven years passed in Gorky. A scientist to the core, Sakharov hit upon the precise image to describe his life: "I feel like a mouse in a jar, from which all the air is being slowly pumped." But even in that secluded place, Sakharov began to sense change. The Soviet Union had a new leader, Mikhail Gorbachev, who had begun some modest reforms. His slogans were *perestroika*, restructuring of the old ways, and *glasnost*, a more open government and

PERESTROIKA

GLASNOST

freer expression of ideas. People held their breath, wondering how far these ideas would be put into action. Sakharov wrote to Gorbachev, calling for the release of anyone imprisoned for their beliefs. Then he put it out of mind. All his letters went unanswered.

Ten months later, a knock on the apartment door startled Andrei late at night. A KGB agent and two workmen pushed their way inside. Without a word, the technicians began installing a telephone. Andrei gaped, speechless. At last the agent spoke. "You'll get a call around ten tomorrow morning." With that, they left.

The phone was silent all the next morning. Andrei tried not to keep glancing at it. Nothing, until three o'clock, when a ring pierced the silent apartment for the first time in seven years. Elena stood wide-eyed as Andrei picked up the receiver.

"It's Gorbachev," he mouthed to her.

"I received your letter," said the voice on the line. "We've reviewed it and discussed it … You can return to Moscow."

Was he dreaming? For an instant Andrei wasn't sure. "Thank you," he finally managed. Then he snapped to his senses. He blurted out the names of other political prisoners and insisted they be released, too.

"We've released many, and improved the situation of others," Gorbachev answered, getting a little impatient. "But there are all sorts of people on your lists."

Before the end of the year Andrei and Elena were riding the night train to Moscow. He stepped off the train in the early morning, still tall but his face much thinner now, his eyes still kind beneath the huge fur hat he had started wearing in frigid Gorky. He could tell immediately that the country had changed. The platform was packed with journalists, foreign and Russian.

Andrei Sakharov and Elena Bonner, after Sakharov's return from exile

After years of isolation, he was bombarded with people who wanted to talk to him. He met with foreign leaders, and was excited to talk about science with British physicist Stephen Hawking. All his former honors were returned, and new ones added. At the Institute, tears welled in his eyes when he found his name, now faded, still on his office door.

The Soviet Union collapsed, and Russia moved closer to democracy. Many of the things Sakharov fought for became reality: greater freedom to travel, freedom of expression and of religion. World destruction by nuclear weapons is no longer the imminent threat it was during the Cold War, though danger remains as long as the weapons exist. And injustices still plague Russia. Sakharov would have expected as much. He came to realize that the fight for human rights is ongoing, no victory final.

FREEDOM OF EXPRESSION AND OF RELIGION

"The future can be wonderful," Andrei Sakharov said, "but it might not be at all. That depends on us."

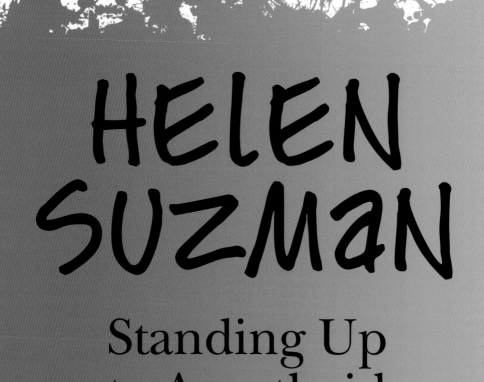

HELEN SUZMAN

Standing Up
to Apartheid

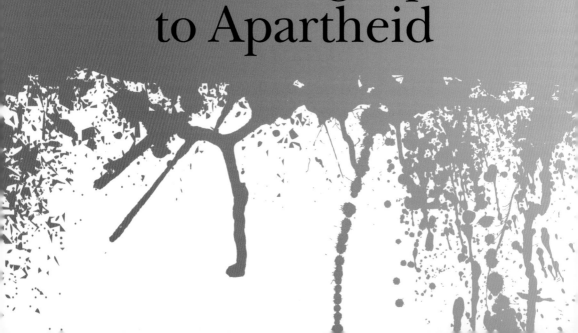

South Africa, 1967

A lone woman gripped the railing as the ferryboat lurched over the waves. The other passengers had retreated inside the cabin. Cape Town was behind them; ahead, across the choppy, freezing water, lay an island with a sinister reputation. It held a maximum-security prison. Surrounded by shark-infested waters, nearly nine kilometers (five and a half miles) from the mainland, it was known to be escape-proof.

A lot like Alcatraz, Helen Suzman thought, tightening her grip as the boat crested another wave, and wishing she'd brought seasickness tablets. Still, she didn't want to miss the first glimpse of the fortress that held the man she had at last been allowed to visit, a man her country had condemned to life in prison. His name was Nelson Mandela.

Half the inmates on Robben Island were political prisoners—convicted of sabotage, treason—and none of them were white. In prison, like everywhere else in South Africa, the lives of blacks and whites were strictly separate. As a white woman, Helen was breaking taboos coming here, but she'd heard rumors that Mandela and his fellow prisoners were treated harshly. And as a Member of Parliament, she had special permission to investigate. Didn't that also make it her duty? She may have once looked the other way, long ago, but that was over. Never again would she turn a blind eye to injustices others wanted to hide.

How would the prisoner feel about seeing her? They were so different from each other, and yet strangely alike— both rebels, both striving to change South Africa in ways others would fight to the end to resist.

SURROUNDED BY INJUSTICE

If Helen Suzman had a stubborn streak, she certainly knew where she got it from. From her youngest days, her father, a Jewish immigrant who had escaped oppression in Lithuania, had taught her to persevere. Helen never knew her mother, who died shortly after she was born. Growing up motherless, she learned early to take care of herself.

As a child, Helen never knew any black South Africans other than those who did chores at her house. At twelve, she signed passes to give one of the family servants, a grown man, permission to be out after 9:00 p.m.

When she was sixteen, Helen went to university to study commerce. She traveled in Europe, and at nineteen, she married Mosie Suzman, a doctor. Soon their family included two daughters.

South Africa fought alongside the Allies in World War II, and there was great celebration when the war ended. But Suzman was troubled by sinister trends at work in the country.

POVERTY The gulf between rich white South Africans and poor blacks was widening. Suzman grew uneasy with the contrast between that poverty and her own life of privilege. Others seemed to ignore it, but she couldn't. What she saw of black South African life nagged at her conscience. How was it any different from the abuse her father had suffered? And how could she just go on enjoying her easy life?

South Africa's National Party, with its firm belief in apartheid, came to power in 1948. Helen was more worried than ever—many National Party members had embraced Nazism and its racist ideas during the war. But she and her husband, Mosie, loved their home too much to leave.

The new government passed one law after another that confirmed her fears. Helen complained bitterly to close

SOUTH AFRICAN APARTHEID

*A*partheid means "apartness" in the Afrikaans language. Apartheid was the slogan and policy of the National Party that came to power in 1948. It extended and legalized the separation of blacks and whites that already existed in the country.

By the 1950s, all South Africans were classified according to race, and laws set out where each group could live and do business. As a result, nearly 80 percent of the land was preserved for the white minority. Apartheid laws discriminated against black South Africans in many ways, and kept them from participating in government. The inequality led to growing tension and violence in the country, but South Africa's government refused for decades to change.

A typical apartheid sign, in English and Afrikaans, warns black South Africans to stay out of whites-only areas.

friends. Unless every South African had the same rights, their beautiful country would become a shameful tyranny. Her heart sickened to see it. "Why don't you run for Parliament?" one friend suggested, as the 1953 election approached. *Ridiculous!* Helen thought, but when she told Mosie, he looked serious and said she should.

I'll never win, she told herself, *so there's no harm trying*. But, to her surprise, she won the seat for a wealthy suburb. She set off for Parliament—sixteen hundred kilometers (a thousand miles) from her home in Johannesburg—to be a back-bencher in the United Party, the Official Opposition. In her suit and pearls, her wavy light hair brushed off her face, she tried to look fearless. "Who am I kidding?" she whispered to herself. "I'm shaking in my boots. It's a fluke I'm even here."

She was one of only a handful of women Members of Parliament, and many male MPs believed a woman's place was at home with her children. But she wasn't going to let that hold her back, or ever show them how scared she felt. She labored over her speeches, making sure everything she said was backed up by hard, researched facts, so no one could trip her up or humiliate her. "Helen, you've got a man's brain!" one MP said cheerfully, thinking he'd handed her a compliment. "His was not a brain I admired," Helen said when she told the story.

JOINING FORCES

The government continued to drive a wedge between blacks and whites. They proposed new laws to force the separation of races in all sorts of public places: waiting rooms, parks, washrooms. To Suzman's horror, the United Party opposition decided to support the new laws. Members of her party were supposed to stand up against the government's excesses, and here they were behaving like its puppets!

As a United Party member, she was supposed to vote along with her party. But she could never support such laws—she had come to Parliament to stop this kind of injustice. She refused to vote, and amid gasps, walked out of Parliament. A newcomer, and she had acted with open defiance! *Now I've done it*, she thought.

Black South Africans, though denied voting rights, were also struggling against the system. The group known as the African National Congress (ANC) was the greatest force for change. In 1959, members impatient with the slow progress against apartheid decided radical action was the answer. They broke away from the ANC and formed the Pan Africanist Congress.

Suzman knew what this meant: violence would break out sooner or later. Whenever she had the chance to stand up and address Parliament, she delivered a warning: the government's actions were making people desperate. But her cries fell on deaf ears. Her own party refused to do anything. She soon realized she was surrounded by people terrified of any change that might threaten the power and privileges whites enjoyed.

"This is it," she blurted out to her friend Kathleen, as they left Parliament one night. "I'm resigning. I'm not staying in a party with this disgusting attitude."

Her friend nodded. "I'm with you."

Helen noticed a group of United Party members, heads together, talking. She tugged Kathleen's sleeve and the two walked over. "What's up?" Helen asked. It turned out they were resigning, too. The whole group talked late into the night. No one wanted to stay in a so-called opposition party that never opposed anything, but giving up rankled them all.

"Let's form our own party," Helen suggested. A vote was taken and the majority was in favor. Suzman and eleven others formed the Progressive Party. It would be openly and strongly anti-apartheid.

The new "Progs," as the others nicknamed them, got a cold reception from Parliament. They were banished to basement offices and treated like outcasts. But for Helen, the strong team spirit made it bearable.

A CRISIS ESCALATES

Of all the apartheid laws, Suzman despised the Pass Laws most. Blacks who came for jobs in the cities had to get temporary permission to work there, but could not move to live near their jobs. They had to carry passbooks that showed they were allowed to be in restricted, whites-only areas. Any black person found without a passbook in a white area could be arrested. Helen now shuddered whenever she remembered signing passes for her family's worker when she was a child. She could hardly believe she had once accepted it as normal. Now she saw the laws for what they were: a way of using black people's labor while denying them the right to choose where to live.

PASS LAWS

"Burn your passbooks!" the Pan Africanist Congress leader declared to black South Africans in 1960. In Sharpeville, just south of Helen's hometown, a crowd of protesters headed to the local police station to hand in their passbooks. One police officer panicked and fired his gun into the crowd. Immediately other officers began to fire, killing some sixty-nine protesters and injuring many others. What became known as the "Sharpeville Massacre" inspired protest marches and strikes throughout the country. "Now they'll have to change those horrid Pass Laws!" Helen said to Mosie.

But she was wrong. In April the government declared a state of emergency. It was now illegal for large groups of people to meet, both the African National Congress and the Pan Africanist Congress were banned, and the minister of justice was given power to imprison people without trial. Soon sixteen

A South African man displays his passbook.

Helen Suzman

hundred people were locked up, and the number of arrests would quickly pass eleven thousand.

In Parliament, only Suzman and the handful of Progs stood up to oppose the government's actions.

"Take away people's hope for change," she warned, "and they will believe there is no choice left but violent resistance. Do we want to drive desperate people to that conclusion?"

"Any concerned MPs may visit the prisoners," was all the minister of justice would concede.

BEHIND BARS

Suzman and a friend drove to Pretoria to visit those in jail. The clang of the iron door behind her was a sound she would never forget, and the sight of the bars and gray cells would haunt her. In front of Suzman, the commanding officer warned the prisoners that they could give her messages for their families, but they weren't to discuss conditions in the prison.

"You mean I can't tell Mrs. Suzman we're on a hunger strike?" a prisoner asked.

"No, man, you can't tell her that," the officer replied.

Helen kept a straight face as the prisoners continued to reveal all.

Back in Cape Town she delivered a speech in Parliament describing the prisoners on hunger strike. Newspapers were forbidden to publish many things under the state of emergency, but parliamentary speeches were an exception. The story quickly made headlines. Now Helen understood she had two weapons against 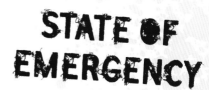 apartheid. Being an MP could get her into places the government would rather hide. And in Parliament no one could silence her, while the press could print her words. She started using both.

In 1961, an early election was called—partly because of the terrible events in Sharpeville. Twenty-six Progs campaigned hard to be elected as the voice of human rights in government. But as the results trickled in, it became clear only one Prog was going to return to Parliament: Helen Suzman.

"Ma, what are you going to do?" her daughter Frances asked, amazed.

"I don't know," Helen said honestly. She now faced an onerous battle: fighting apartheid in Parliament, without a single ally.

CARRYING ON ALONE

Munching a sandwich at her basement desk, Helen thought of the United Party and National Party MPs all lunching together in the private dining room above. She'd never felt so lonely. She closed her eyes and pictured her dad. He wouldn't have given up. Then she pictured other faces—the ones behind bars in the Pretoria jail. *So many black South Africans fighting for change, risking their lives to do it. What I have to put up with is nothing compared with their lot*, she thought, slightly ashamed. She pushed her self-pity aside. She'd use all her time alone to hammer out speeches that would make the government squirm. Her new tactic was both simple and

FIGHTING FOR CHANGE

relentless: whenever a minister delivered a speech, she seized her right to question him, but her questions were about the treatment of blacks, their slums, the brutal treatment of those arrested. The exchanges were often printed in newspapers, both in South Africa and abroad.

"You put these questions to embarrass South Africa overseas!" one minister blurted out, exasperated.

"It is not my questions that embarrass South Africa—it is your answers," Helen shot back.

Her opponents accused her of having a secret army of speechwriters working for her—how else could she challenge everything so tirelessly, always with facts at her fingertips that exposed every weakness? Helen rolled her eyes. "If only it were true!" she lamented to her daughter.

Suzman's sharp tongue became notorious. National Party MPs fought back, unafraid to attack her with any means. She was dismissed as a chattering woman, called a lunatic, even accused of buying votes with bottles of brandy! Helen seethed, but refused to be lured into shouting or saying something that could be used against her. To her opponents, she showed a tough exterior, as hard-skinned as an armadillo. Her doubts and fears she kept to herself, or confided in Mosie, so far away at home, in late-night calls. The hate mail began to pour in, from anonymous writers who accused her of ruining the country. She bought a whistle to blow into the ears of nighttime callers who tried to frighten her.

A WARNING

There could be no backing down. A new outrage was in full swing: the forced removal of black and other nonwhite city dwellers to designated "homelands," often far away from their actual homes. Families were being broken up, and the awaiting towns were unprepared for the flood of newcomers. Mere survival there was a challenge.

"People are dropped out on the grasslands in midwinter with a tent they don't know how to erect, without doctors, schools, or even clean water!" Suzman protested in Parliament. She was starting to feel like the only MP with eyes to see what was all around them. How could the whole Parliament be blind? *Was* she as crazy as they said? She later visited a black township at the plea of a priest. Conditions were even worse than she had feared. *No*, she thought, *I'm not the crazy one.*

Houses in an apartheid-era township in one of South Africa's homelands

The African National Congress formed a military wing, Spear of the Nation. Its leader was Nelson Mandela. Frustrated with the lack of progress moderate black leaders were making with the government, Spear of the Nation prepared for armed action. Mandela and others were arrested.

"Always," Mandela said in his own defense at his trial, "we have been conscious of our obligation as citizens to avoid breaches of the law, where such breaches can be avoided; to prevent a clash between the authorities and our people, where such a clash can be prevented; but nevertheless, we have been driven to speak up for what we believe is right, and work for it and try to bring about changes which will satisfy our human conscience. Government violence can only do one thing, and that is to breed counterviolence." At her first opportunity, Suzman read his words in Parliament.

BRING ABOUT CHANGES

Ignoring the warning, the National Party government sped headlong on its path toward the violence Mandela described.

A SINGLE "NO"

In April 1963, the Ninety-day Detention Law was brought before Parliament for vote. It would let any commissioned officer imprison people without a trial, even if a state of emergency had not been declared. Helen listened to the leader of the Official Opposition criticize parts of the bill. Then, to her shock, he announced that his party would vote for it. The Speaker invited any response from another MP. No one moved.

If I don't stand, Helen realized, *no one will*. She had no carefully prepared speech this time—she would have to wing it. Helen got to her feet and just started talking.

"Long before the final chapter of the struggle that is

going on in this country is written," she began, "a great number of people who were formerly peace-loving will be driven to desperate acts of recklessness." She felt like an engine building up steam. "Government members should imagine themselves in a black skin for one day of their lives, and let them see whether it's easy to get a job, to move freely around the country of their birth, to live where they wish to live, and to have their family live with them."

At last she sat down, quaking not with nerves, but with outrage.

A vote of "Aye" and "No" was taken. A thundering chorus of "Ayes" was followed by Helen's lone "No."

"I think the 'Ayes' have it," the Speaker said dryly.

Helen couldn't believe it. A violation of a basic human right was going to be passed in *her* beloved country's Parliament. She stood up again, all eyes on her. "Divide!" she called.

It was her right as an MP to insist that everyone take a side, literally. The bells rang for three minutes, calling any absent MPs into the room, and the doors were locked. Then the Speaker stood up and put the question of whether the law should be passed. "Those in favor take seats to the right, those against to my left."

The entire Opposition streamed to the right, where they joined the National Party MPs. Helen looked at the vacant green benches around her, stretching out like a sea. She was utterly alone.

VOICE OF THE VOTELESS

Helen Suzman's lone opposition to the bill caused a scandal. Angry people accused her of protecting murderers and violent criminals, of ruining South Africa. Enraged MPs called her "the biggest political enemy of this country!" But by this time, Helen's already thick skin had hardened to armor. No insult seemed to rattle her. Inside, she was still afraid she might fail, but to the world she acted as though she were invincible.

A long list of parliamentary votes followed, with Helen Suzman the only opponent of measures designed to enforce apartheid. The government argued that these tools were necessary to maintain order—black rebels were inciting riots, arming themselves, and threatening chaos! Helen thought of the words of British statesman William Pitt the Younger, words she'd known since school. "Necessity is the plea for every infringement of human freedom. It is the argument of tyrants; it is the creed of slaves."

BIGGEST POLITICAL ENEMY OF THIS COUNTRY!

Letters kept flooding in, but they were not all hate mail. Helen was heartened by how many writers thanked her for speaking for those without a voice—she felt less alone. She also got letters pleading for help from people forced out of their homes, or unable to visit their children in jail. Again, Helen felt the pang of knowing how much more black South Africans risked in this struggle than she did. Thousands turned to her for help. The *New York Times* declared that "as the sole voice of the voteless, she actually represents more South Africans than all the other members of parliament combined."

A FIRST MEETING

In 1964, Nelson Mandela was sentenced to life in prison for plotting military action against the government. He and his fellow defendants were sent to the impenetrable Robben Island. Rumors that he and others were abused there reached Helen Suzman, and she asked the minister of justice to let her visit him. During the ferry ride she steeled herself for what she might see on the forbidding-looking island.

The commanding officer of the prison was waiting for her when she arrived. Solemnly he walked her to the single-cell section, where thirty men were to spend their lives in hard labor, breaking rocks and collecting seaweed. Helen subtly noted everything as she passed, and the conditions worried her.

Robben Island's sun-bleached quarry, where prisoners labored

She stopped at the first cell, but her cheery hello was interrupted by the inmate. "Don't waste time talking to us. Go and talk to Mandela at the end of the row. He's our leader."

Helen continued down the row to the last cell and peered through the bars on the door. Inside stood a very tall, upright man, waiting. Even in prison garb and behind bars, he looked like a man in charge. Before she could speak, Nelson Mandela passed his hand through the bars. "How do you do, Mrs. Suzman. I'm very pleased to meet you."

"How are things here?" Helen wasted no time.

"They are very bad indeed," he said frankly, ignoring the commanding officer's presence.

Mandela calmly listed the problems he and the other prisoners faced. The guard in charge had a Nazi swastika tattoo and had promised to make their life hard—which he did, whether they were breaking stones in the quarry or sleeping on the floor on thin bedrolls. The food was inadequate and visits were rare. Suzman promised to take up his concerns with the justice minister.

She left, deeply impressed by Mandela. Not long after, she got a call from Mandela's lawyer. "Nelson Mandela asked me to thank you—the guard has gone." But when she asked to visit again, she was turned down. Suzman applied to visit Mandela every year—only an annual visit was allowed—and was denied permission seven times.

When at last she was allowed to return she was relieved to see that conditions had improved. She stubbornly kept returning. *The authorities need to know someone is watching*, she thought, *and the prisoners need to know someone outside cares.* Her persistence made a difference. The next time she arrived, one prisoner grinned. "We knew you were coming!" he said. "When the sacks of fresh peas arrived this morning, we knew it must mean a visit." Whenever the food suddenly improved, or people sleeping on the floor were suddenly given beds, prisoners looked at each other and said, "Auntie Helen!"

Mandela was moved to a less harsh prison on the mainland, where Suzman kept visiting. They became friends. His plight was becoming famous, partly thanks to her efforts, and countries around the world pressured South Africa to free him. Suzman knew her first impressions of Mandela had been right: he was a good leader and, amazingly, had grown not more radical in prison but more patient  and peaceful. He now saw clearly that black South Africans had to work with the whites, not against them, to change the country. "A university for leaders," Helen called Robben Island, only half-joking.

The outside world began to condemn apartheid and pressured South Africa to abandon it. South Africa had been barred from the Olympics since 1964, and the United Nations denounced apartheid in 1973. Yet at home Suzman was still accused of being the champion of those who broke laws and

created chaos. Among the whites, her main allies were a handful of reporters who wanted change, and people abroad. As she prepared to leave for New York to be honored for her struggle for human rights, a minister sneered: "The Honorable Member is going to America tomorrow to receive an award from people who are South Africa's enemies."

"You leave us with no friends so I have to accept awards from our enemies," Helen snapped.

PROMISING SIGNS

In 1974, a new election was coming, and after thirteen years as the only Progressive MP, Helen Suzman made up her mind. She would resign if she was the only Prog re-elected. The strain of working alone was finally exhausting her. Maybe no one wanted her after all, and it was time to accept it.

On election night she and her volunteers sat in a school hall for the vote count. Her pile was rising; it looked as though she would win. A window opened and a head popped inside. Helen recognized the friendly face of a Prog supporter. "We've won Johannesburg North!" he said. Helen shook her head. "I don't believe it." *Two* Progs in Parliament?

But it was true. As the night wore on, others ran in to announce one Prog win after another. Five more seats altogether. To any other party, five seats would be nothing to celebrate. But Helen and the volunteers hugged one another and jumped up and down. After thirteen years, she was no longer alone! Winds of change had surely begun to blow if voters were sending six anti-apartheid MPs to Parliament.

The change that election night seemed to promise was agonizingly slow. In 1978, P. W. Botha became prime minister, and later state president. He made some reforms, struck down the Pass Laws, but went no further. Suzman debated him fearlessly, and while he thought she was on the side of lawbreakers, he grudgingly admired her. "She's worth ten United Party MPs," he remarked. "*That's* an understatement," she quipped.

SMASHING APARTHEID

Suzman visited Nelson Mandela again in 1986, after waiting for permission for two and a half years. They talked now about forging a new future for the country. She had imagined that all the years in prison would have battered Mandela's spirit. But the opposite was true. Suzman came away certain that this was the person who could both persuade the African National Congress to avoid violence and speak to the government with enough calm authority to negotiate.

AVOID VIOLENCE

In 1989, F. W. de Klerk became state president, and his opening speech to Parliament stunned Suzman. It was his aim "to realize full civil rights for all South Africans." That year she decided to retire. She was seventy-two, and had been an MP for thirty-six straight years. She was confident there were enough others to carry out the final victory. In her farewell speech, she directed her remarks at the new president, letting him know she thought the time to smash apartheid was now.

NEGOTIATE

"As an old African saying has it: 'You should not argue with the crocodile if you are still in the water.' The state president designate, is, I believe, no longer in the water. He has both feet on the banks of the river and he is in no danger of being dragged down by the crocodile. He should now go for it."

One year after Helen Suzman retired, de Klerk's government freed Nelson Mandela and legalized the African National Congress and other opposition parties. Mandela became president of the ANC. By working with the white government, promoting the interests of all minorities and not just black South Africans, he angered some of his followers. But the rest of the world was encouraging. In 1993, Mandela and de Klerk together won the Nobel Peace Prize for their efforts. And the following year excitement filled the nation as South Africa held its first elections by universal vote—black, white, and every minority. Helen Suzman was on the commission that ensured the elections were fair. Voters swept Mandela and the ANC to victory.

Nelson Mandela
and Helen Suzman

A rocky road lay ahead for South Africa, as it would take time to mend the damage done by apartheid, but the country was on the right course at last. Helen Suzman's courage was of a special kind: the heroism of endurance. She waged a struggle for thirty-six years—thirteen years alone—against what she knew was tyranny, while a vast majority rejected her. It always amazed Helen that those years in prison never did wear down Nelson Mandela's spirit. And yet she was similarly undefeated during her own decades-long struggle.

MEND THE DAMAGE DONE BY APARTHEID

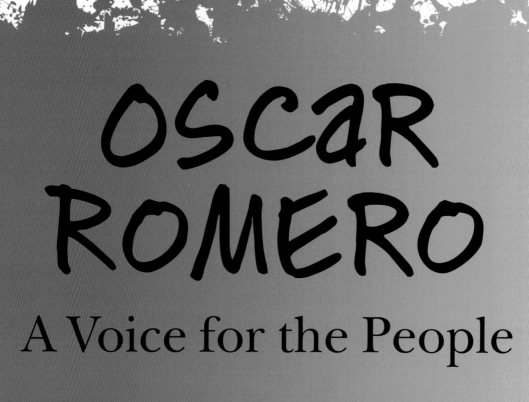

OSCAR ROMERO

A Voice for the People

El Salvador, 1977

A crowd of thousands filled the cathedral—the huge building could not contain such a sea of people, who flowed out its doors and covered the steps and plaza outside. Archbishop Oscar Romero had declared that one single mass would be held on this Sunday—a symbol of unity among the people of El Salvador and an urgent call for change. And the turnout today was massive. Millions more listened on radio. To Romero, the message was clear: the people were united, and they were behind him.

He had been archbishop for less than a month; only a week ago he would never have considered such a bold action—a direct challenge to the rich and powerful, in a country plagued by injustice. But the terrible events of the past few days had opened his eyes. The time to speak out was now.

After mass he looked down to see his hands trembling. They shook almost constantly now. He had seen a doctor about it, but the problem was not a medical one. Romero was discovering he was a strong-willed leader, yet before now he had always humbly obeyed his church. The two sides, the leader and servant, were at war inside him.

When Romero was chosen to be archbishop, the army generals and rich landowners had smiled with satisfaction. In a country where most people were Catholics, they needed him to be an ally. "He's so cautious and old-fashioned—he'll never challenge us," they said. "He'll stick to sermons and stay out of politics." Priests who'd been helping peasants fight injustice were bitterly disappointed. This timid, intellectual man would never help them.

The generals and the priests couldn't have been more wrong.

EL SALVADOR

El Salvador is a small, Spanish-speaking country in Central America. From the late 1800s, a small class of "coffee barons" grew very wealthy there, exporting the country's coffee beans. Owners of sugar cane plantations made similar riches. The rich landowners depended on huge numbers of *campesinos*, peasant farmers who harvested the coffee beans and sugar.

The owners felt threatened by peasant unions, which might demand that the workers share the profits of the harvest. They also feared that the millions of peasants might rebel and install a communist government, which would seize their land and their wealth. When in 1931 El Salvador's military commanders took over the government in a coup (a sudden, violent seizure of power), most landowners approved. A right-wing, military regime would prevent their fears from becoming reality.

El Salvador's landowners counted on the military to protect their wealth and control the country's peasants.

FINDING HIS CALLING

One early morning in 1930, a boy climbed onto a mule and began a long journey down twisting trails. He was leaving his family and his mountain village, perched high above the hot, humid plains. Its cobblestone streets and adobe houses were always cool, far from the heat and bustle below. It would take the boy seven hot hours to reach his destination: the seminary at San Miguel. His father wanted him to be a carpenter, but at thirteen he knew he wanted something else: to be a priest.

At the age of twenty-four, his face browned by the sun, with its square jaw and eyes peering seriously from behind glasses, Oscar Romero donned the long cassock of the priesthood. To his fellow priests he seemed quiet and calm. When he did speak, he was direct and honest. Inside, Oscar demanded a great deal of himself. He scolded himself for being too timid, and kept a diary to note his failings and the ways he must improve. If only he could be more at ease with others, he wrote.

He soon made a discovery. When he preached to a crowd at mass he always knew what to say. Standing before many, his words took flight; he was fiery and inspiring.

In 1974, Romero was named bishop of Santiago de María, and he tackled the job with energy. He noticed that many peasants weren't coming to mass on Sunday, and found out why. The dirt roads from their faraway villages to the cathedral were so bad they were staying home. So he set out in a jeep with loudspeakers, preaching, and stopping here and there to baptize babies. Being out among people made him happy and full of zeal.

THE GATHERING STORM

All around him were signs that the country was in trouble. The military and the wealthy landowners feared one thing above all: a revolution among the peasants who worked the land. And even worse than peasants who talked rebelliously were the priests who helped them organize and demand better wages. The military government declared any kind of peasant union or group to be illegal.

Oscar, for all his eagerness to help, was traditional at heart. The Church, he believed, should stay out of politics, as it always had, and concern itself with the spiritual life of the people—teach them to lead good lives, bring them closer to God. In fact, wasn't it holy to accept suffering? His respect for authority ran deep. It was simply wrong to challenge those above you.

One day, parishioners ran to tell Bishop Romero that government troops had attacked a group of local peasants. Romero rushed to comfort the families, and in his next sermon he condemned violence. Then he hesitated. He knew so little of the peasants involved—what if they were criminals? If he sided with them, he might embarrass the Church. So his next step was to write a respectful letter about the incident to the president. *It must have been the act of a few bad soldiers*, he thought. *Surely those in charge will fix things.*

On another occasion, Romero was shocked when someone else told him that the coffee plantations weren't paying pickers minimum wage. "But these are good people!" he exclaimed, amazed. He knew these landowners—they would come to mass, shake his hand. In his parish newspaper, he simply asked that the wealth of the coffee harvest be shared with all. Migrant workers arrived to pick the coffee beans, and he let them sleep in the cathedral, and made sure they ate a hot meal. He wanted harmony, not conflict. Yes, life was hard for so many, he said to himself, but real liberation was spiritual, not worldly.

HARMONY, NOT CONFLICT

"SPEAKING THE TRUTH"

In February 1977, Oscar Romero was made the new arch-bishop of San Salvador, the head of the country's Catholic Church and leader of its millions of Catholics. He had not been everyone's favorite candidate, but he was the first choice of powerful people who feared change. Surely he would reject radical priests who championed the demands of the poor; he'd force them back into line or else disown them.

The ceremony was short and simple: Church leaders felt times were too dangerous and tense for the delay a grand occasion would cause. Priests who sided with the poor against the ruling class had been expelled from the country for "sedition." A growing number of people were being "disappeared"— arrested and never seen again. Peasants were organizing illegally. Guerrilla groups were arming themselves to fight

Archbishop Oscar Romero

the government. Election campaigns for the presidency were in full swing, and rumors spread that the election would be fixed. It was said that General Carlos Romero (who was not related to Oscar) would be declared the winner, no matter how people voted.

On February 26, the government indeed announced that General Romero would be the next president, once outgoing President Molina handed over power. The evidence of voting fraud was overwhelming. The following day sixty thousand people were protesting in the main square of the capital, San Salvador, when government troops opened fire on the crowd.

Archbishop Romero was horrified, but unsure what to do. He met with the country's bishops. "We must speak out about these outrages," he declared. They argued with him. Breaking off friendly relations with the government would bring worse troubles. Only one bishop sided with Romero.

"This isn't about breaking relations," Bishop Rivera cried. "It's about seeking and speaking the truth! The people expect the Church to speak on their behalf, and it must do so."

Rivera's boldness gave Archbishop Romero the courage

he needed. Together they wrote a protest. They denounced the shootings and disappearances, the exile of priests, and the poverty that most Salvadorans suffered. Romero would read it at two masses on Sunday.

The day before he was to deliver his protest, Romero was paralyzed by second thoughts. It was too harsh and would inflame tempers; the timing was wrong. Rivera argued with him. "Well," said Romero at last, "I'll read it at the mass in the cathedral, but not in San José de la Montaña." That second mass would be filled with rich landowners.

Rivera sighed, but said nothing about Romero's apparent cold feet. "If you read it in the cathedral, it's broadcast by radio, and that's enough." The Church's radio station always broadcast Sunday mass and classical music.

A TURNING POINT

That night Romero's phone rang. It was President Molina, calling to offer his condolences. Romero listened in shock. Father Rutilio Grande had been traveling from one village to another, with an old man and a boy from his parish. Between the fields of tall sugar cane that flanked the dirt road, all three had been found shot. There were no witnesses.

THE MURDERS MUST BE INVESTIGATED

At last Romero recovered his voice. The murders must be investigated, he demanded. Molina promised to find the killers.

As Romero hung up the phone, he felt everything had changed. The next morning he read out his protest against the government's violence and indifference to the poor—at both masses, before rich and poor alike. Then he put away his notes and spoke from his heart. He mourned not just the three victims, but all those who had died and disappeared.

He called upon the murderers, who might be listening to the radio in their hideout, to repent their actions.

Romero's about-face shocked everyone. But for him, it was as if he saw clearly for the first time. The Church's greatest duty was to defend the weak. How could he have been so blind? He'd been afraid of "political" priests, but hadn't he taken a political side when he'd supported the government by standing by and doing nothing? That was over. His faith was meaningless if he did not take action in the world.

Romero now hounded the president to investigate the murders. Molina made more promises, but with no result. He implied that the killers might be enemies of the government, who wanted to blame him and throw the country into chaos. *If that's the case*, wondered Romero, *then why doesn't the government try harder to find them*? Never again would he blindly believe whatever people in power told him.

Romero decided to close all Catholic schools for three days and on the next Sunday have only a single mass, in the cathedral of San Salvador. One common mass would be a powerful sign of unity among the people. Those who couldn't attend could listen on the radio. He called a meeting of priests and put it to a vote—he must not impose his own will without one. They overwhelmingly agreed.

Landowners and the papal nuncio, the Pope's representative, were furious. How dare Romero release Catholics from their duty to go to mass? Or stage a public protest? The Church must stick to the middle and not choose sides. But Romero stood his ground. And on Sunday, he was convinced he'd been right. One hundred thousand people turned out for the single mass, crowding the cathedral and its plaza.

STAGE A PUBLIC PROTEST

THE PEOPLE'S CHAMPION

In April, a small rebel group kidnapped the foreign minister, demanding for his ransom the release of political prisoners. Romero pleaded for his life, appealing to the kidnappers in the newspapers. He offered to act as mediator. But the government refused to negotiate, and the minister was found dead in May. At the man's funeral, Romero condemned all violence, the violence of oppressors and equally the violence of those who rebelled against them. And he continued to call upon the president to fulfil his promises and investigate all the deaths.

To the government, Romero was now an enemy. The state-controlled newspapers began to publish attacks on the archbishop. He aided terrorists, they declared; he condoned violence. He sheltered revolutionaries who called themselves priests. His own church rejected him, they proclaimed. Romero was unshaken. He held fast to the revelation that had changed his life: the Church *was* the people, especially those fighting for freedom.

Thousands came to hear Romero preach, and millions of Salvadorans listened to him on the Church's radio station. The government might control newspapers and TV, but Romero could still use the station to get the truth out. He started getting letters from peasants, many written by the one

person in a village who could read and write, his signature surrounded by dozens of thumbprints, showing the support of his neighbors. They told Romero about arrests, intimidation, and trying to live good lives while surrounded by persecution. Some said they had never felt the Church was close to the poor before now. Romero was deeply moved by their messages of encouragement: "We are not frightened by so many threats," one letter declared, "the more we are threatened, the braver we feel, and therefore we write you not to feel alone."

UNDER ATTACK

Among Romero's own bishops there were those who resented his bold actions, and now they attacked him, saying that he was being used as a political pawn and was too foolish to see it. They called him a meddler: "You're dividing the country. You've confused the nation!" Bishop Rivera stood by Romero.

Many of Romero's bishops might be against him, but he knew he had the unswerving support of the priests and the poor of El Salvador. He was also encouraged to learn that news of what was happening in his country was spreading to other parts of the world. A delegation from England visited El Salvador and reported back home on the human rights abuses they saw there. Romero hoped this international spotlight would help. His friends, like Bishop Rivera, hoped it might protect his life. So many opponents of the government had simply disappeared—what really stood between Romero and that fate? Would his high profile be enough to protect him?

The rumors spreading about him among Church leaders

troubled Romero. He had never stopped wanting to be loyal to his church, and it hurt to have that loyalty questioned. He decided to go to Rome and defend his actions before the Pope.

As soon as he arrived at the Vatican, a powerful cardinal loudly scolded him for becoming a political agitator. Then he told Romero to wait; the Pope would speak to him privately. Romero steeled himself for what was to come. He thought of himself, still a boy, riding the donkey down the hillside, leaving his home and family, because he wanted to be a priest and dedicate his life to the Church. Had he strayed too far from his calling? Were his motives pure? As always, he prayed to find the answers, and felt stronger. He would simply tell his story.

The Pope listened, then took the photos of the murdered priests from Romero and looked at them. "Courage," he said at last. "You are in charge." Romero felt a burden had been lifted.

TAKE REAL ACTION

HOPES RAISED

Back home the crisis escalated, but now Romero felt calm. His hands had stopped shaking. Now that his purpose was clear, his energy was boundless.

In October 1979, two military officers came to visit Romero one evening. They had important news that must be kept absolutely secret. They were part of a large group in the army plotting to overthrow the government. Many officers had decided that President Romero was not dealing with the crisis in the country. Together they would force him to step down.

"We'll take real action to end the country's problems," they vowed. "We'll bring about land reform that will be fair to all."

"But will you investigate the deaths, the disappeared, all the human rights abuses?" demanded Romero. The officers promised they would. "Promises must be backed up with actions," Romero reminded them. He did not give the plot his blessing, but he was hopeful.

The coup took place with lightning speed, and the president fled into exile. The new government was made up of both civilians and army officers. It seemed like a good sign that people outside the military were finally sharing control of the country. The new leaders announced their good resolutions and made some progress: a human rights commission was created and land reform was underway. But their changes did not go far enough. To Romero's deep disappointment, injustice continued. Within three months the civilians had resigned from the government, having found it impossible to control the arrogant military. Once again, the powerful army was completely in charge.

People's hopes of true change were dashed. Violence flared up again. In his radio sermons, Romero begged all sides for patience and restraint. In secret, members of guerrilla groups who wanted to wage war on the government visited him. He pleaded with them to abandon their violent tactics, but always found them unchanged in the end.

REFUSING TO BE SILENCED

In February 1980, a powerful bomb destroyed the Church's radio transmitter, and Romero's voice was off the air. Word spread of the sabotage, and donations to build a new transmitter poured in, mostly from the poor. Romero was driving one day when a taxi pulled up alongside. The driver waved to him eagerly, and Romero lowered his window. "For the radio!" the taxi driver shouted, handing him a few coins.

The following Sunday, the cathedral was packed with people holding up tape recorders so they could spread Romero's message themselves. Romero appealed to the authorities to end the violence. "Let them not keep on killing those of us who are trying to achieve a more just sharing of the power and wealth of the country. I speak in the first person, because this week I received notice that I am on the list of those who are to be eliminated."

His friends knew he'd been threatened before, but he'd never spoken publicly about it. This was serious. In fact, the nuncio to Costa Rica had warned Romero that his life was in danger. Romero's small house, next to the cancer hospital, seemed like such an easy target that he started sleeping in his old room behind the hospital chapel's altar. The foreign minister of Nicaragua offered him a safe haven in his country. Romero refused. He could not leave his people; he would accept alongside them "the risks of the moment."

When the rebuilt radio station was back on the air, Romero spoke longer than he ever had. As always, he listed many incidents of violence, so no crime could be buried

Romero's house, on the grounds of a hospital in San Salvador

under lies. Again, he appealed to those in power, and to soldiers themselves not to carry out evil orders. "No one has to fulfil an immoral law. It is time to take back your consciences … In the name of God, and in the name of this suffering people … I beg you, I beseech you … stop the repression!"

STOP THE REPRESSION!

He had promised to say a mass at the cancer hospital chapel the next day. Romero's friends at the hospital told him they were worried. The mass had been announced in the newspaper, mentioning that Romero would be there. It was too dangerous, too unprotected. Couldn't someone else say the mass? Romero wouldn't change his mind.

He took his place behind the altar, facing the small group that had gathered. "One must not love oneself so much," he said to them, "as to avoid getting involved in the risks of life that history demands of us … those who try to fend off the danger will lose their lives … the grain of wheat … dies, but only apparently … only in undoing itself does it produce the harvest." As he finished his sermon, a gunshot sounded, ear-splitting in the small chapel. Romero fell to the ground.

For a moment people froze; some ducked down in their pews. Then, panic-stricken, they fled the chapel. A few ran against the crowd toward the altar. Behind it they found Romero lying unconscious. They lifted Romero, carried him to a truck outside, and drove him to the hospital. He died shortly after.

THE PEOPLE GRIEVE

Two days later, Romero's body was carried in a silent procession, followed by thousands, and laid in his cathedral. For a week, crowds filed past his body from early morning until night. As the day of the funeral mass approached, grieving

Crowds gather outside the cathedral for Romero's funeral.

priests and nuns hung a banner over the entrance, declaring that the government and the bishops who had failed to stand by Romero should all stay away from the funeral. Bishop Rivera was the only Salvadoran bishop at the funeral mass, but bishops from over a dozen other countries came. Despite the huge crowds, no police or soldiers were to be seen, and everything went ahead calmly, at first.

Suddenly a bomb exploded in the plaza outside the cathedral. In almost the same instant, shots were fired, and the thousands gathered began to scream and run, some into neighboring streets. Others ran up the cathedral steps, rushing over the iron fence for the doors, and trampling one another in the panic. Inside the cathedral, the crowd huddled, waiting for the shots outside to stop.

In the afternoon the government announced that a rebel group had set off the bomb, then held people hostage inside the cathedral. Yet witnesses had seen someone shooting from a window of the National Palace, and were sure the bomb had come from there, too.

A LEGACY OF HOPE

In the days that followed, rumors spread about who had killed Romero. It was the work of the military, some said. They did it to start riots so they could attack the protesters. Some said anti-government extremists had killed him, hoping to make him a martyr. No one at Romero's last mass had seen the killer. Whoever it was had fired through the open door at the back of the chapel and quickly fled. In the first moments all anyone cared about was saving Romero if they could.

The government promised to investigate, as they had so many times before. For a long time the truth seemed impossible to find. The friend who had asked Romero to say the mass remained convinced that El Salvador's police had killed him. The judge assigned to investigate the killing fled the country after a man shot at him in his home. Would Romero's murderers never be found, and had Romero become like the victims he had championed—whose attackers were never brought to justice?

HE DENOUNCED INJUSTICE AND ABUSES AGAINST HUMAN RIGHTS

Over the next years, likely suspects within the military began to emerge. In 2004, a judge in California found Captain Alvaro Saravia, who had been living there, liable in a civil suit for Romero's death. Saravia remained in hiding.

Bishop Rivera succeeded Oscar Romero as archbishop. He pointed to one clear reason for Romero's murder: "He denounced with inexorable vigor institutionalized injustice and abuses against human rights. This gained him the esteem of those near and far, but it also aroused the animosity of those who were vexed by the force of his ... word ..."

The injustices Romero exposed were seen by the rest of

In 2007, demonstrators in El Salvador carry on Romero's struggle for justice. Their banner declares "Romero Lives!"

the world, and it became impossible for the government to keep hiding its crimes. Still, the path to freedom would be long and difficult: twelve years of civil war followed the coup that ousted President Romero in 1979. Then came promising signs. In 1990, the United Nations mediated a peace treaty in El Salvador, ending the fighting.

The government of El Salvador is now elected democratically, but it faces huge challenges: poverty, crime, and a country still divided between rich and poor. Yet today basic education is free, and poor children receive shoes and uniforms. These are the kinds of hopeful signs Romero spoke of two weeks before he died: "If I am killed, I shall arise in the Salvadoran people. I say so without boasting, with the greatest humility … Let my death … be for my people's liberation and as a witness of hope in the future."

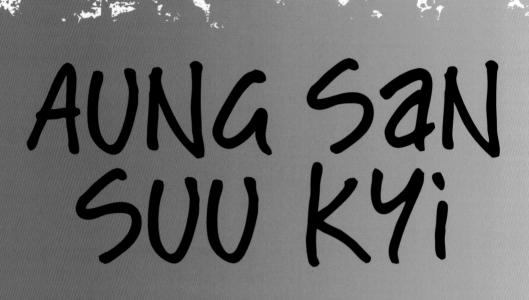

AUNG SAN SUU KYI

Prisoner for Democracy

Slowly, Suu Kyi mounted the platform they had built for her on the grounds of the Shwedagon Pagoda. That golden Buddhist shrine, with its gleaming peaks, seemed to wrap protectively around her. Before her was a crowd of thousands, waiting. They had come to hear her, or at least to see her. She'd had no time to get nervous on the way; it had been too much of an ordeal just to get through the teeming crowds to her destination. But now, for an instant, she paused. Who was she, after all, to be telling the people of Burma what to do? A revolution had begun, but might soon be crushed by a brutal regime. What answers could she give those expectant faces? She had been away for so long, would not even be in the country now if her mother hadn't needed her.

She raised her eyes and gazed at the huge portrait of her father that someone had placed on the platform, honoring him as one of Burma's greatest heroes. Suu Kyi drew a deep breath. She may not have chosen this path, but it had been given to her and no one else. She took her place before the portrait, turned toward the sea of faces, and told them the truth.

HOMECOMING

The airplane descended through the clouds, and a familiar land came into view for the passenger watching through her window. It had been years since she'd seen her homeland, Burma—or Myanmar, as the military regime now called it. She had lived abroad for much of her life, in India and then in England, where she studied at Oxford, and where she met and married her English husband. In that faraway country she'd heard the news that her mother was very ill, probably dying. Now she was coming home to be with her.

Suu Kyi's thoughts traveled back to her first memories, images of her father. She pictured herself running downstairs when he came home, how he would pick her up. Had that really happened? People had told her so many stories about her father, she couldn't be sure. He was a hero in Burma, the man who united a country finding its independence after more than sixty years of British rule. His charisma brought people together. But Aung San was shot and killed by a bitter politician when Suu Kyi was two years old. As she grew up, she quietly pieced together the story of his life, learning all she could about this father whose portrait seemed to be in every home, even printed on their money. Barely remembering him, she nevertheless loved and admired him.

The plane touched down outside the capital, Rangoon, and slowed to a stop. Along with the other passengers, Suu Kyi rose, small and delicate, graceful in her movements. People who met her called her serene. Only some detected the

Rangoon (Yangon), Burma

People Who Said No

BURMA/MYANMAR

Bordered by India, China, and Thailand, Burma (also called Myanmar) has a long and turbulent history. For a thousand years Burma was a powerful country in southeast Asia, ruled by kings who waged wars of conquest. Buddhist monks were important leaders and royal advisors.

The British, who wanted to trade in the area, fought the Burmese and colonized the country in 1885. The king was exiled. After World War II, Aung San was key in negotiating with England for Burma's independence.

A civilian government was formed in 1948, and Burma was a republic until a military coup in 1962. The generals who took over claimed they were saving the country from disintegrating because of its rebellious minorities. Today, one half of the population lives at or below the poverty line. Most people live in fear of the military authorities. The ruling regime has used the official name Union of Myanmar since 1989. Many of those who oppose the regime still call the country Burma.

Suu Kyi's father, Aung San, who helped Burma achieve independence from Britain

strength behind her cool exterior. That strength was about to be tested to the extreme.

At the hospital, Suu Kyi's reunion with her frail mother was bittersweet. A stroke had made it impossible for her mother to hug her, but she was still alert, and her eyes shone when Suu Kyi came to her bedside.

Suu Kyi spent her days visiting, and every time she walked through the hospital, she was shocked by what she saw. The rooms she passed were crowded with wounded young people, most of them students. They were being treated for gunshot wounds, broken bones. She began talking to the students' friends, come to visit, just released from arrest. Their stories alarmed her.

There had been student protests against the military government, she learned, a groundswell beginning at the university in Rangoon and spreading across the country. The trigger had been the sudden devaluation of Burmese currency—overnight, money wasn't worth the paper it was printed on, and it was the corrupt military regime's fault. The students were demanding democracy and a return to civilian government. But the crackdown was swift and brutal. Riot police and truckloads of soldiers had opened fire on the protesters, scattering the screaming crowds. Now the universities were closed, and curfews kept everyone indoors at night. Trucks with loudspeakers drove through the empty streets, blaring their grim message in the eerie silence: *Stay inside or be shot on sight.*

CORRUPT MILITARY REGIME

"But are you really Aung San's daughter?" one student after another asked Suu Kyi, amazed to see the child of their hero in person.

Suu Kyi listened to their stories with concern, but she kept her thoughts to herself. In Oxford, Burma's problems

In 1988, pro-democracy demonstrators clashed with the regime's soldiers.

had seemed so far away! She felt herself blush at the memory of her own small plans to help her country: maybe start a library or a student exchange with England. No, something far greater was needed here. But what could she do? She had responsibilities: now forty-two years old, she had two sons back in England, waiting, along with their father, for her to return. So she listened, saying little, only asking each person how she could help in practical ways. "Just like her father," older people began to say, nudging one another.

A LEADER FOR THE CAUSE

Within a couple of months it was obvious that Suu Kyi's mother would not recover. Suu Kyi took her to their family home to spend her last days. Her husband, Michael Aris, and their sons, Alexander and Kim, arrived, too. They weren't the only visitors. Fifteen-year-old Alex was baffled by the steady stream of people who came and chatted for hours—all types, from students to eighty-year-olds. The house had become a hub of revolutionary plotting. Over and over, visitors urged Suu Kyi to take a stand in the crisis. She stayed cautious.

What can be done, she wondered, *without causing any more violence? And what can* I *do?* She couldn't find an answer.

In August, nearly four months after Suu Kyi's arrival, a young university teacher named Nyo Ohn Myint came to visit her. Within moments of meeting her, he knew she was "a people person," someone others would follow, including himself. He got right to the point. "The movement needs a leader," he said bluntly.

SPIES EVERYWHERE

Suu Kyi shook her head, and Nyo Ohn Myint left, disappointed.

Her father was the hero, not her, she told herself. She was just in Burma for her mother, for a little while. What about her brother? But he was living in the United States, and had no longing, she knew, to return.

Over the next days, stories of more army violence against protesters reached Suu Kyi at her mother's bedside. It was too much to bear. And as if on cue, Nyo Ohn Myint came back. This time, Suu Kyi told him she was ready to help, but she refused the title "leader." "A temporary coordinator," she suggested. *That's a start*, Nyo Ohn Myint thought, nodding. He pledged himself to help her, as did several of his students.

A mass rally was planned for August 26 at the city's golden Shwedagon Pagoda. Suu Kyi agreed to speak to the crowd, but in the days leading up to the event, she grew anxious. The regime had spies everywhere, and they had learned of her plans. Soldiers started bullying people, discouraging them from going. Pamphlets appeared everywhere, insulting Suu Kyi and hinting that she would be assassinated at the Pagoda.

Shwedagon Pagoda in Rangoon (Yangon). This sacred building is an important Buddhist pilgrimage site.

A stubborn pride was kindled inside her. She wasn't going to back down in the face of crude threats. She asked the students if they would come as bodyguards—but unarmed ones. A dozen jumped at the chance to show their loyalty.

HOPEFUL CROWDS

On the day of the rally they set out in a convoy of eight cars, each one carrying a woman and a bodyguard. Despite the threats, a crowd of hundreds of thousands was waiting. Suu Kyi had never expected such huge numbers. Many had camped overnight to be near the podium.

Suu Kyi climbed the steps, glancing up at the portrait of her father on the platform. She stood before it, looking small and slender in her traditional Burmese high-necked jacket and long skirt.

"Reverend monks and people!" she began. The noisy crowd fell silent, and Suu Kyi felt the weight of their expectations on her. The mere fact that Aung San's daughter was before them was enough to raise excited hopes.

She began by honoring the students who had started the fight for democracy. Then, knowing the weaknesses her enemies could attack, she proclaimed them herself. Yes, she said, she had lived most of her life outside Burma, and she had married a foreigner. But that didn't mean she knew nothing of Burma's problems.

"The trouble is, I know too much. I could not, as my father's daughter, remain indifferent to all that is going on."

Her next words surprised many. "Let me speak frankly. I feel strong attachment to the armed forces. Not only were they built up by my father; as a child I was cared for by his soldiers." But the military must answer to a government of civilians, elected by the people, she said. She made it clear her goal was not to overthrow, but to reconcile. When she finished, the applause was thunderous. From then on, she became widely known as Aung San Suu Kyi, combining her father's name with her own in a most unusual way.

RECONCILE

That crowd of hopeful faces made up her mind. She would stay in Burma until democracy was achieved.

THE PLOTS OF GENERALS

People gathered for peaceful demonstrations, and instead of breaking them up, the regime lifted martial law. It amazed everyone that the army's iron grip appeared to be loosening. Hopes were high: democracy was in reach! Suu Kyi and Michael guessed it might take a few months, maybe a year.

To Aung San Suu Kyi's dismay, the demonstrations turned into looting. The whole movement was chaotic, she realized, without real leadership, but she also suspected the regime was behind the sudden mayhem. She was right—in secret meetings the generals had plotted to send trouble-makers into the demonstrations, planting the seeds of violence everywhere. They released criminals from prison and bribed them to commit arson. If the chaos grew, the generals reasoned, everyone would beg the army to quell it.

Soon the generals seized their chance to restore order. General Saw Maung proclaimed an emergency cabinet of senior army officers. The State Law and Order Restoration Council, SLORC, was created. This clique of generals would now rule Burma and control the "mobs" that threatened peace. They had the blessing of Burma's previous military ruler, who had retired that summer. The names had changed, but the military was still in charge—and had granted itself new powers of suppression. Widespread arrests of the demonstrators followed. Aung San Suu Kyi's home filled with people talking anxiously about the news. She stepped away from the arguing voices and sat alone, sunk in thought, a frown etched on her brow. For the first time, she saw how terribly deep Burma's troubles were.

Then to everyone's surprise, the new SLORC regime announced a promise. No date was given, but there would be

"free and fair" elections. It seemed too good to be true. Would they keep their word? Aung San Suu Kyi wondered. What were they up to?

BRAVING INTIMIDATION

On a September afternoon Suu Kyi looked out the window of her mother's house and quickly drew back. Soldiers swarmed outside. Nyo Ohn Myint hurried to her side to see for himself. In no time it looked as though a hundred soldiers were surrounding the gates at the entrance to the grounds. Jeeps with mounted guns were parked outside.

Suu Kyi looked quizzically at Nyo Ohn Myint. He hated to tell her what he suspected. He'd heard that some of the radical students wanted to stage their own coup and declare themselves the government until the elections. Aung San Suu Kyi may have refused the role of leader, but she was already a powerful symbol for many. SLORC must have reasoned that she was at the center of the rebellion.

Aung San Suu Kyi went outside to confront the soldiers at the gate. "No one may come or go," was all they said.

OFFER NO VIOLENCE

Nyo Ohn Myint roamed the house looking for something they could defend themselves with. All he found was a ceremonial samurai sword the Japanese had given Suu Kyi's father. Hardly useful! He drew Suu Kyi aside. "We could make Molotov cocktails, in case they storm the doors."

"No!" she snapped. They would offer no violence, even in self-defense. "It is better that I be taken off to prison. It is better that we should all be taken off to prison." If they used force, Suu Kyi insisted, even a little, they would betray their principles.

Two days of suspense followed. The third morning, a student peeked through the curtains and said, "There are

Aung San Suu Kyi

fewer soldiers than before!" They continued to drift away. Aung San Suu Kyi breathed a sigh of relief.

A LEAGUE FOR DEMOCRACY

"How long will you stay in Burma?"

Aung San Suu Kyi had lost track of how often she'd heard the question, and it was starting to make her angry. "I'm going to stand by the democratic movement here all the way," she answered, checking her temper. Only her clenched fists gave her away.

As for the mystery behind the promise of an election, the regime's reasons were becoming clear. Other countries had denounced the State Law and Order Restoration Council for stifling the democratic movement, and had stopped investing in Burma and sending aid. Now the country was bankrupt and desperate, and the government was selling Burma's precious tea, gems, and oil to anyone who would pay. The only way to restore aid was to convince other countries that Burma was a fair democracy after all.

The new regime was also arrogant. The generals believed that their new party, the National Unity Party (NUP), would win—intimidation and propaganda would sway voters, they were sure. After all, Burma had only a single national newspaper, and it was under the regime's control. Nothing could be published, not even a leaflet, without SLORC permission. And gatherings of more than five people were outlawed. Who could compete with them?

Yet, strangely, they encouraged people to form political parties for the upcoming elections. New parties were rewarded with telephone lines and gasoline, luxuries that were hard to get. This, undoubtedly, was also part of their plan. So many people would scramble to start parties, they reasoned, that it would be a confusing mess, and NUP would win. In the worst case, the generals said, there will be no clear winner at all. Then the military would step in to restore order, again.

The SLORC generals were right about the rush to form parties: 234 new parties eventually registered. Having already dipped her foot in the water, Aung San Suu Kyi now took the plunge. She formed the National League for Democracy

(NLD) with Aung Gyi and U Tin Oo, two defectors from the old regime. The party would be broad and inclusive, welcoming minorities who were often ignored. It mixed former military and civilians. Aung San Suu Kyi still shied away from calling herself a leader, and she agreed to be third in charge. Yet it was obvious hers was the name that made people flock to the NLD.

A steady stream of visitors came to see her, some just to spend a few moments with Aung San's daughter. She could sense quickly what someone wanted, and she made people feel listened to. At her home, she was constantly surrounded by young people and students.

Aung San Suu Kyi felt grateful to the students. They were the ones who'd led what everyone was calling the People's Revolution. And she trusted the young. They were honest and open about their goals and plans.

THE PEOPLE'S REVOLUTION

But she was worried. She knew there were some around her who were radical at heart. Among the students, some still talked of taking the country by force, then holding elections. Aung San Suu Kyi knew that was no answer. It would only be replacing one violence with another. "That cycle must end with us," she would say.

BRUTAL TACTICS

In the midst of the turmoil, her own life reached a crisis. Her mother died, and Aung San Suu Kyi quietly grieved. Her husband and sons, their visas expired, prepared to leave the country. After an inner struggle, Suu Kyi told Michael she was staying behind. She knew SLORC hoped she would leave with him, but there was too much still to be done. Michael agreed, though his face was grim. Once they had left, she felt terribly alone. But she vowed to keep her personal pain to herself—why add to the burdens others were already carrying? To those around her she acted energetic and untroubled. They had, after all, an election to win.

"Talking to people in Rangoon is not enough," she said. "We have to get out and meet people around the country." It was crucial to cover ground before the monsoon made villages impossible to reach.

SLORC fought her campaign from the start. Soldiers came to rallies, guns at the ready, to intimidate the crowds. While she spoke, nearby army trucks blared loud music, making it hard for her to be heard. Locals were warned to stay away, but thousands still turned out to hear her speak, many wearing broad-rimmed peasant hats to hide their faces from government spies. The hats became a symbol of the National League for Democracy.

When Aung San Suu Kyi and her team drove into the village of Danubyu to give a speech, she knew right away something was wrong. The village seemed deserted. Only soldiers stood on the street corners. In the town center, a few

villagers stared at them, but there were no cheers, only chilling silence.

An army captain approached Suu Kyi as she stepped from her car. The village was under martial law, he told her. There would be no speech. He didn't tell her that the villagers had been warned not to come greet her, and that those who did would be shot.

Suu Kyi was fuming. *They want to silence me with intimidation, and scatter our supporters*, she thought. But she couldn't hand SLORC such an easy victory. "We'll continue with our plan," she said to the others. The group began walking to the waterfront, where three boats were to take them to villages along the river. Suu Kyi held her head high, pretending not to hear the jeers and shouts of the soldiers they passed.

They returned late in the afternoon. As their boat neared the dock, they saw soldiers crowding the waterfront.

"Let's keep going along the river," one student whispered. Aung San Suu Kyi shook her head. Any change in their plan was a win for their enemies.

The soldiers along the dock raised their guns. "Do not land," the captain's voice boomed over a loudspeaker.

"Ignore him," Aung San Suu Kyi said. "I'll land first." She stepped off the boat and walked past the soldiers.

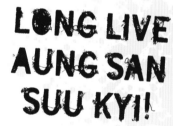

The group set out slowly, soldiers flanking them and following like stalking cats. The short walk seemed to take forever. From somewhere in the silent village, a voice called, "Long live Aung San Suu Kyi!"

Ahead they saw a line of troops kneeling, guns aimed at them. Aung San Suu Kyi turned to the others behind her and told them to stop. Only she, and one student who refused to leave her, would risk walking farther.

They heard the captain's voice again. "If you do not go back to your boats, you will be shot!"

The captain ordered his men to fire on the count of three. Aung San Suu Kyi's companion halted and closed his eyes. She silently stepped around him and continued forward, alone.

YOU WILL BE SHOT!

"One! Two!' the captain counted.

Another voice boomed. A major shouted at the soldiers. They lowered their weapons. Aung San Suu Kyi kept walking.

Had it all been a mere show of force by SLORC? Aung San Suu Kyi did not know. Every move of the regime's forces was cloaked in secrecy. What she did know was that today she had won.

THE CAPTIVE

It was early on a July morning in 1989 when truckloads of soldiers again pulled up before the gate of Aung San Suu Kyi's house. She ran outside, but was turned back at gunpoint. No one would be allowed to leave or enter, the commander said. She glanced up and down the street. Barbed wire was strung across either end, blocking the way. She hurried back inside to reassure her sons, who'd been allowed in the country to visit.

Hours passed. Alexander and Kim hid any fear they felt, playing cards and board games. Suu Kyi tried to call Michael in Scotland, but international calls had been barred. Over the past few days, one NLD member after another had been arrested. Was she next? Would they take her to prison?

Ten hours crawled by, with no answer. At 4:00 p.m. two officers came to the gate. "May we come inside?" they asked with careful politeness. Aung San Suu Kyi stepped forward to face them.

"You are under house arrest," one of them said. "You cannot leave the house and grounds, cannot contact anyone from NLD. The regime will decide who can visit you. A maid and cook may stay, but everyone else—besides your sons—must go."

If I protest, Suu Kyi thought, *the soldiers will surely break inside.* There were forty people with her—her sons, loyal students, and they could be hurt.

She asked the others to go home. Reluctantly, they filed out. The soldiers then entered and fanned out through the empty rooms, searching every cupboard and drawer. During those first moments, Suu Kyi overcame her shock. Now she was able to stand by, her face serene. She even smiled a little. *They'll find nothing to incriminate me*, she thought. *Not a single illegal object or printed word.* The search ended with the frustrated soldiers leaving empty-handed.

Her captors announced that she had been put under house arrest for "committing acts designed to put the country in a perilous state." Her house arrest would be for one year, but it could be renewed. She did have a choice, the officers hinted slyly. She could leave the country now, with her sons, and not come back.

"The only way I will leave Burma," she said, "is if I am taken to the airport in chains."

She sat down between her sons, her hands shaking with anger. It was amazing how little the regime understood her, if they thought she would leave. *But then*, she realized, *that's the arrogance of rulers who completely ignore the people they abuse. They don't take the time to understand anyone. They think everyone can be bought or bullied.* Instead, she demanded to be taken to prison, just like the rest of the NLD. Her captors refused.

A BRIEF REUNION

In Scotland, Michael found out about Suu Kyi's arrest on the radio, and rushed to Burma. The regime allowed him to enter. Clearly, they hoped he might convince his headstrong wife to leave with him, and their troubles would be over. As soon as his plane landed it was surrounded by soldiers, and Michael was whisked away. He was being taken to Suu Kyi, they told him. He would have two weeks with her, but if he spoke to anyone from an embassy or the NLD, he would be thrown out of the country at once.

No one would know where he was, Michael realized. It would be as if he'd disappeared.

September came, and the boys and their father had to leave. Even apart, they would pull through as a family, Michael encouraged Suu Kyi. The elections would come, and then democracy. It wouldn't be long before they'd be together again.

On their way out of the country, the boys were forced to surrender their Burmese passports. They would not be allowed back. It was an obvious ploy to push Aung San Suu Kyi to her limit. If she couldn't see her children, she might agree to leave forever.

THE PEOPLE VOTE

With Aung San Suu Kyi locked away, her party in prison or scattered, the regime felt safe at last to announce a day for the elections: May 27, 1990.

On May 26, the few NLD members who were still free drove through Rangoon, encouraging people to vote. In the morning the turnout was massive. People stood patiently in the long lines that snaked away from the polling booths, eager to cast their ballots.

The wins for each seat were announced as they were counted, with the final, official result to be declared June 14. The results that trickled in were the opposite of what SLORC had expected. NLD candidates were winning seat after seat. Soon it was obvious that Suu Kyi's league for democracy had been chosen by the vast majority.

SLORC stalled in announcing the winner. Inside her house, Suu Kyi waited in suspense. At last the regime spoke. The ballots had been tampered with, they said. In any case, SLORC was the recognized leader of the country and nothing obliged them to give up power. They would, however, begin a transition to civilian government. Once the army agreed, a new constitution would be drawn up and put to a referendum. They gave no hint as to when this might happen.

HOPES OF A FAIR ELECTION

Protesters took to the streets, but were brutally suppressed. All hopes of a fair election were dashed.

Had she stayed for nothing, then? Suu Kyi pushed that thought away, as she also struggled with the longing to see her sons. She kept the image of their faces bright in her mind, told herself they would be together again, and did not dare ask herself when. And she waited.

LOCKED AWAY, BUT NOT FORGOTTEN

At the end of Suu Kyi's year of house arrest, her heart sank when she was told it was being renewed for another year. She had secretly feared this. They could keep her there indefinitely—even for the rest of her life.

In the home that was now her prison, Suu Kyi turned to Buddhism for comfort and wisdom. She kept to a disciplined routine to stay sane. Each morning she meditated—as so many NLD prisoners did, to keep their minds sharp during the lonely hours in their cells. Then she gave herself chores. At first she'd gone outside to work in the garden, but when she saw soldiers photographing her, she turned and defiantly went back inside. *They won't take my privacy, too*, she vowed, and she let the garden grow into a tangled jungle around her walls. She read and played the piano until it went out of tune.

She covered her walls with quotations about freedom by Gandhi and her father. Her guards glanced at them, smiled, and said nothing. That was when she made a decision. She would treat the soldiers assigned to her with respect. It wasn't their fault, and Buddhism taught her to care for all beings. *Metta*, loving kindness, would be her guiding principle. The guards were surprised when she asked them about their families and got them smiling again. Suspicious that they were growing too friendly, their commander replaced them. Again and again.

MAHATMA GANDHI

Mohandas Karamchand Gandhi, known as Mahatma ("great soul") Gandhi, was born in 1869 in India, which was then ruled by Britain. He devoted much of his life to leading the struggle for Indian independence.

A deeply spiritual political leader, Gandhi is most admired for his use of nonviolent protest to change unjust laws or social inequality. By refusing to cooperate with injustice, he believed, a person proclaims the truth. This noncooperation can take the form of boycotts or civil disobedience.

Although many found this philosophy too idealistic, under Gandhi's guidance the strategy won major victories in India, where it was used to challenge British authority and laws that discriminated against Indians. Gandhi lived to see India achieve independence in 1947.

Mahatma Ghandi, whose commitment to nonviolent protest served as an inspiration to Aung San Suu Kyi

At night, unable to sleep, Suu Kyi slipped downstairs and looked at the photograph of her father. Suddenly she felt very close to him. "It's you and me, Father, against them," she whispered.

SLORC hoped to make Aung San Suu Kyi disappear. The regime made it a crime to own her picture or even say her name. Her father's picture was removed from the currency. Her supporters began referring to her simply as "The Lady," but soon even that was too dangerous.

Yet SLORC's plan backfired. Instead of disappearing, Aung San Suu Kyi was turning into a symbol of freedom in Burma, and a famous prisoner of conscience around the world. The United Nations condemned Burma's military rulers and called for her release, as did the United States and other governments. In Europe, Suu Kyi was awarded the Sakharov Prize for Freedom of Thought. (In 1988, the European Parliament created this human rights award and named it after Andrei Sakharov.) After two years of house arrest, she was awarded an even greater honor: the Nobel Peace Prize.

In Burma, the award changed nothing for the imprisoned Suu Kyi. She heard the brief noise of crowds celebrating outside her home, then shuddered at the screech of army trucks and the sound of booming voices on loudspeakers as soldiers arrived to scatter them.

FACING THE WORLD AGAIN

On July 10, 1995, a white limousine drove up to Aung San Suu Kyi's house. She'd had no warning of a visit, and she looked out the window a little apprehensively. She had been a prisoner in her home for nearly six years.

The city's chief of police stepped out of the vehicle and walked to her door. To Suu Kyi's disbelief, he told her in a polite voice that she was no longer under house arrest.

No warning and no explanations either! SLORC was just as mysterious about their reasons for letting her go as they were about all their motives. International pressure for her release may have become too great. Or perhaps SLORC had become arrogant again. The NLD was so weak by this time, how could Suu Kyi make any trouble for them?

Thousands gathered outside her house when the news spread. To her old friends she seemed calm and collected, as mentally tough as ever, but her body was frail now. Was she strong enough to face the crowd outside?

They set up her desk behind the iron gate, and cheers erupted when she finally appeared, standing up on it. Democracy was still possible, she declared, but it was necessary to stand up for it, and be patient.

The crowds kept coming. Soon a ritual developed. Each weekend she would stand up on the desk, her head peeking over the gate, her hair always adorned with jasmine or orchids. She would joke with the crowd, and answer the letters that had been crammed into her mailbox. Military spies roamed

through the crowd. People could pick them out by their sunglasses and frowning faces. But there were no soldiers.

She had preached "freedom from fear" as one of the greatest goals for the Burmese. Now she seemed to have achieved it herself. When people worried about her safety, she said, "If the army really wants to kill me they can do it without any problem at all, so there is no point in making elaborate security arrangements."

A HEARTBREAKING CHOICE

A couple of weeks after her release, to Suu Kyi's joy, her husband and son Kim were allowed to visit her. But after that, their requests to come back were refused. Then, in January 1999, Michael called Suu Kyi with terrible news. He had been diagnosed with cancer and his chances of recovery were very slim. Yet he was not allowed to come to see her.

She had to leave at once to be with him! But they both knew that she would never be allowed back in Burma. "Stay," Michael insisted. While she was there, she was the champion of so many people in prison and their families. What would happen to them if she left?

Her enemies in the government had always slandered her in the state newspaper. Now they denounced her for abandoning her husband and sons. The accusation stung, but as always Aung San Suu Kyi kept her pain to herself. "I dream about my family all the time," she did say once, "but there are a lot of people here who need to be cared about and loved and looked after. They've become my second family."

Michael died two months later, and the authorities then let Alexander and Kim into Burma, for the first time in three years. Suu Kyi was shocked at how much they had changed from the images she had treasured in her mind. They were young men now. "I wouldn't have recognized Kim if I'd passed him on the street," she whispered to a friend. The visit flew by, and she watched them go, not knowing this time if she would ever see either of them again.

Still, she kept her personal struggles private, and she threw herself into work with the NLD. The regime's soldiers harassed her. Police roadblocks barred her way when she tried to drive out of Rangoon. They were just protecting her, they said, from terrorists. *So*, she thought, *I'm free, but on a very short leash.*

Enough was enough. Aung San Suu Kyi announced in public that she was leaving Rangoon by train with her fellow NLD members. At the train station she was swarmed by soldiers and pushed into a van. They drove her to her home. She was back under house arrest.

THE STRUGGLE CONTINUES

Life under house arrest continued off and on for years. A brief period of freedom, a stint in military prison, but then back to the villa. International calls for her release increased. Music stars dedicated songs to her. But Suu Kyi's isolation deepened. No visitors anymore, not even her sons. No letters or books. The world wondered about her.

NO LETTERS OR BOOKS

Why did they keep her alive? Were they using her as a bargaining tool, holding on to her so foreign governments could be coaxed with promises of her release?

The clamor around the world grew too loud to ignore. Now the regime announced that multi-party elections would take place in 2010. Would they be fair? Would the winners actually be able to shape the country's future, or would the military continue to pull all the strings? People held their breath, afraid to be as hopeful as they'd been in 1990. So did Suu Kyi, alone in her crumbling villa.

In May 2009, Suu Kyi was shocked to hear that she was being charged with breaking the terms of her house arrest. No visitors were allowed, but an American who was a stranger to her had broken the rules by swimming across the lake near her compound and entering the grounds. Suu Kyi was convicted, but allowed to serve her sentence where she was, still in her house. Nothing changed for her, but she guessed that the trumped-up charge had one purpose: to prevent her from taking part in the elections.

In 2007, demonstrators in London, England, wear masks with the face of Aung San Suu Kyi and tie their hands to protest her house arrest.

Her fears were confirmed in March 2010. New election laws were announced: no one convicted of a crime could participate. And no one who had married a foreigner could run for office. They weren't taking any chances: Aung San Suu Kyi must be kept out of the elections altogether.

Her supporters at the NLD were outraged. In protest, they refused to register their party under the new laws, and the National League for Democracy disbanded. The regime's party faced little opposition on November 7, 2010. Their candidates were swept to victory, despite loud accusations of fraud in the voting.

Six days later, another polite official arrived at Aung San Suu Kyi's gate to release her from house arrest. Their election victory in hand, the military rulers felt it was safe to let her out. Then the year 2011 brought surprising signs of hope. The NLD re-entered politics. Aung San Suu Kyi was invited for talks with the regime's president.

Some Burmese fear that Aung San Suu Kyi is too idealistic. Only bold action, they say, can change Myanmar. But like Gandhi and Martin Luther King Jr., both leaders Suu Kyi admires, nonviolence is at the very heart of her beliefs. Any new order brought to power with violence, she believes, will soon resemble the dictatorship it replaced. And then the cycle of violence will continue.

NONVIOLENCE MEANS POSITIVE ACTION

"I do not believe in an armed struggle, because it will perpetuate the tradition that he who is best at wielding arms, wields power," she says. But nonviolence is not passive, either. "Nonviolence means positive action. You have to work for whatever you want."

A revolution, she insists, must be more than a change in material conditions. It must be "a revolution of the spirit."

UPRISING iN EGYPT

A People's Revolution

Cairo, Egypt, 2011

"Go! Go! Go!"

Tens of thousands of voices, their day-long chanting reduced to one simple demand. The voices came from a crowd that had taken over Tahrir Square, a busy traffic junction in the center of Cairo. The target of their outcry was Egypt's president, Hosni Mubarak, in power for nearly thirty years.

It started with a message spread on the Internet: Facebook pages called for a "Day of Rage" on January 25. The messengers were mostly young university students. The online response was staggering: eighty thousand people promised to march and add their voices to the others demanding immediate reform. But would they actually show up and brave Egypt's notorious riot police?

To the shock of the doubters, many did. Some thirty thousand people filled streets in the capital, Cairo, and in Alexandria on the coast. They began with a list of demands. End the Emergency Law, which gave police the power to arrest and detain anyone they wanted to, without a good reason. Raise the minimum wage—one in five Egyptians lived in poverty. But by the afternoon it had all boiled down to one urgent call: the president, and his absolute hold on power, must go.

Nothing like this had happened in three decades. It was a sign that things were truly different now. A spirit of revolt was growing in Egypt's young generation, and it would soon spread to other Arab countries—a revolt against strict authority that claimed to know best, and did not answer to the people for its actions.

EGYPT
THE SEEDS OF REBELLION

With about 82 million people, Egypt is the most populous country in the Arab world. Its main religion is Islam, with a small Christian minority. Since the 1950s, Egypt had been typical of its part of the world: a country ruled by strongmen and their security forces, backed by a rich business elite loyal to the rulers.

In theory, Egypt was a democracy with regular elections. Yet Mubarak was often called, in whispers, its "modern pharaoh." A former air force general who became vice president, he came to power in 1981 after President Anwar el-Sadat was assassinated. In the following thirty years, his regime made it almost impossible for any opposition party to get elected. Many Egyptians lived in poverty, while corrupt officials exacted bribes. Common Egyptians had no voice in how their country was governed.

At the same time, Egypt was an ally of Western countries such as the United States. It was one of only two Arab countries to recognize Israel as a nation.

Hosni Mubarak

LIFE UNDER MUBARAK

For so long, it seemed that nothing would ever change. Corrupt officials and police violence were commonplace; low wages made it hard for people to get enough food—and yet they might have to pay bribes just to get a driver's license or to set up a market stall. For years, the main opposition—the only real opposition—to President Mubarak's regime was a group known as the Muslim Brotherhood. But many Egyptians feared they were too idealistic and inexperienced to govern effectively. Given a choice between Mubarak and various revolutionaries, cautious Egyptians stayed quiet and put up with the problems they knew rather than risk facing worse ones. "People survive on a day-to-day basis," said a Cairo lawyer. "They can't go for long without a daily wage and daily bread, so they can't afford to make trouble."

All the while, a huge change was slowly underway. Young people were becoming the majority of the population—soon over half of the people in Egypt were under the age of twenty-five. Many were better educated than their parents, yet they had trouble finding jobs and resented a future that looked so bleak. They expected something more.

The year 2010 brought fresh insults from the corrupt regime. Egypt's powerful police were known to treat citizens brutally. In June, twenty-eight-year-old Khaled Said was beaten to death by plainclothes officers. According to human rights advocates, Said may have had evidence of police corruption. Word spread online. A Facebook page devoted to Said—titled "We are all Khaled Said"—drew 375,000 followers, and quiet vigils were held around the country.

CORRUPT REGIME

In December, elections were held. Mubarak and his henchmen won almost 90 percent of the vote. The fraud was so obvious that no one was fooled. Worse, it appeared that the president planned to force his son on the country as its next ruler.

THE SPARK OF CHANGE

Then, in January 2011, something unthinkable happened. In Tunisia, another North African country with a strict regime, people were flooding into the streets, shouting and protesting. The demonstrations grew so overwhelming that President Ben Ali, who had ruled Tunisia for twenty-three years, fled the country.

WE WON'T STAND HIM ANYMORE

Students in Egypt were amazed, and impressed. If they could muster great enough numbers, why couldn't the same thing happen in Egypt? They began spreading their message on the Internet and mobile phones: "Come together on January 25 for a 'Day of Rage' to show Mubarak we won't stand him anymore."

The tens of thousands who gathered in Cairo and Alexandria were led by students and young professionals who worked in the cities. The regime had the manpower to handle those numbers, and by nightfall the police had taken the public squares back with brute force. What shocked the government was the way protesters had taken to the streets in almost every other city as well, all at once. It seemed the whole country was communicating with a dangerous speed and effectiveness. The regime quickly suspended the Internet and blocked text-messaging and mobile phones. But it was too late.

Over the next couple of days the government seemed frozen. They did nothing. It was as if Mubarak and his men didn't grasp what was happening. In the past, Mubarak had been able to nip dissent in the bud by dividing his opponents. Fighting one another, they never united to take him on. But this time it was different. The Internet campaigns had

Demonstrators fill the streets of Egyptian cities.

reached vast numbers of people who would otherwise never have communicated. Perhaps the regime underestimated how much the Internet had changed Egypt—the days of their controlling all information in the country were over. This movement was bringing together people who might disagree about many things, but were united by a desire for change. They were not from any single group. They were students and teachers, workers and professionals, Muslims and Christians, men and women of all ages and backgrounds.

STANDING THEIR GROUND

By January 28, Tahrir Square was a patchwork of tents, teeming with protesters who were now camping out. Riot police moved in. All over Cairo fights broke out between the riot squads and protesters, and the early scenes of peaceful protest turned ugly. Overturned police cars blazed and tear gas filled the air. Demonstrators were killed; many more were wounded. Yet still the streets did not empty.

Police in Alexandria form a line to block demonstrators, while a few bold protesters approach.

Night fell, and suddenly the riot police retreated, leaving the remaining protesters celebrating. But their disappearance had a dramatic result. Looters and vandals took to the streets, smashing store windows, rampaging through markets. Some breached prison walls, freeing convicts and taking police weapons. Thugs wandered in gangs through poorer areas, terrifying people back into their homes.

Now the sudden retreat of the police looked suspicious. Was this the government's plan? Pull back and let the cities fall into violent chaos? Then the average person would be desperate to have order restored. They would welcome the army. But when the army arrived on the streets of Cairo, something unexpected happened. Many of the soldiers hinted that they supported the protesters, letting them scrawl graffiti on the sides of their tanks—slogans such as "This is a revolution of the people" and "No, no Mubarak." It looked as though Mubarak's show of force was backfiring. Had the army lost confidence in him?

It was after midnight, and after three days of revolt, that the till-then-silent president finally spoke to the country.

On state television, Mubarak said he understood his people's concerns. He would make big changes in government. For the first time he appointed a vice president, and he announced a new prime minister. It was another old tactic: shifting the blame. It had worked before. Fire some ministers, appoint new ones, but hold on to the real power. Protesters were unimpressed. They could see through the charade.

Mubarak added sulkily, "All this opposition has only been possible because I've granted new rights to freedom of expression."

PROMISES ARE NOT ENOUGH

Demonstrations wore on, as did the standoff between Egypt's idealistic youth and their stubborn president.

Until that point, the Muslim Brotherhood had kept out of the way. They'd been threatened with a brutal crackdown and had hesitated to back those calling for the president's resignation. But their younger members were joining the demonstrations on their own, and now the leaders threw their support behind the protesters. They championed Mohamed ElBaradei, a Nobel Prize winner and longtime critic of the government, to negotiate the removal of the president. But still Mubarak clung to power.

Now as well as blocking communication, the government blocked trains and traffic into Cairo, in an effort to halt the flow of protesters streaming into the city. But it was like trying to hold back a wave. In spite of the obstacles, half a million gathered in Cairo, while a hundred thousand more gathered in Alexandria.

Mubarak made his next move. He had never intended to run again as president, he announced, which was certainly news to Egyptians. He would change the constitution—which, as it stood, made it almost impossible for anyone to run against him. He would negotiate with the opposition. Throughout his speech he played the role of a concerned father, saddened by his troublesome children. He also showed his famous stubborn side. "I am a military man, and it is not my nature to abandon my duties," he declared. "I have defended the soil of Egypt and will die on it, and be judged by history."

Only weeks earlier, the promises made by their president would have stunned Egyptians. Now, they were simply not enough.

The regime was a relic; the people had moved on. There was no more patience for "those Stone Age men sitting in chairs," as one young protester called them. The regime indeed seemed deaf to the cries of its own people. And Mubarak's vice president enraged the country's youth when he suggested the protesters' parents should tell their children to go home.

Egyptians of all ages join in the protests.

VICTORY FOR THE PEOPLE

Despite the obstacles, or maybe because of them, people began to band together and cooperate in ways they never had before. In Cairo, where litter usually covers the streets, protesters swept and cleaned the squares they had taken over. Others volunteered to direct traffic and joined together in neighborhood patrols to take the place of the absent police. One young human rights activist found that older Egyptians kept stopping him to thank him, saying, "You have done what we always wanted to do, but never could."

At the end of January, the army's officers had announced that they would not fire on the protesters. The commanders seemed to be in conflict—were they behind Mubarak or not?

The atmosphere of pride and cooperation on the streets was shattered February 2, when pro-government mobs pushed their way into the protesters' camps, starting fights. Some said their ranks included paid criminals and plainclothes government thugs. The armed forces walked a tightrope: protecting the protesters from pro-Mubarak mobs while still asking them to go home.

NEW REFORMS

Revolt had been raging for fifteen days, and all Mubarak would do was promise new reforms. He stubbornly refused to step down. He appeared to be playing a waiting game. If he could just hold out, trading small promises to buy time, the protests might fizzle—or be snuffed out at last by force. On TV, he shook his head sadly, swearing to carry on his duty of taking care of the country. Crowds from Tahrir Square began to march toward his palace.

The military made a decisive move at last. The army declared it was taking action "to protect the nation," and called a supreme military council. Waiting through the night, protesters were confused. What did it mean? The next day it was clear Mubarak had accepted the inevitable. He resigned, handing over power to the military council. They would, they promised, oversee the writing of a new constitution and ensure a speedy return to civilian rule through elections.

In eighteen days, a people's protest had brought down a seemingly invincible regime—against the odds and in defiance of all the pessimists. The dramatic events in Egypt sent waves of revolt through neighboring Arab countries. Protesters took to the streets in Yemen, Syria, Jordan, Iran, Libya, and Algeria. Like Egypt, these countries had large populations of young people. Many of them were educated, yet couldn't find jobs. They were similarly tired of corruption, injustice, and having no voice in their government.

Whatever their outcomes, the uprisings changed people. "I have tasted freedom," a young graduate in Tahrir Square said two days after Mubarak left, "and I will not turn back."

Graffiti on a wall in Alexandria celebrates the protesters' victory.

MAIN SOURCES

THE WHITE ROSE

Dumbach, Annette, and Jud Newborn. *Sophie Scholl and the White Rose*. Oxford: Oneworld Publications, 2007.

McDonough, Frank. *Sophie Scholl*. Gloucestershire, UK: The History Press, 2009.

Scholl, Inge. *The White Rose: Munich 1942–1943*. Middleton, CT: Wesleyan University Press, 1983.

ROSA PARKS

Brinkley, Douglas. *Rosa Parks: A Life*. New York: Penguin Books, 2005.

Parks, Rosa, with Jim Haskins. *Rosa Parks: My Story*. New York: Puffin Books, 1999.

Patterson, Charles. *The Civil Rights Movement*. New York: Facts on File, 1995.

ANDREI SAKHAROV

Gorelik, Gennady. *The World of Andrei Sakharov: A Russian Physicist's Path to Freedom*. Oxford: Oxford University Press, 2005.

Lourie, Richard. *Sakharov: A Biography*. Hanover, NH: Brandeis University Press, 2002.

Sakharov, Andrei. *Memoirs*. New York: Knopf, 1990.

HELEN SUZMAN

Suzman, Helen. *In No Uncertain Terms: A South African Memoir*. New York: Knopf, 1993.

OSCAR ROMERO

Brockman, James R. *Romero: A Life*. Maryknoll, NY: Orbis Books, 2005.

AUNG SAN SUU KYI

Aung San Suu Kyi. *The Voice of Hope: Conversations with Alan Clements*. New York: Seven Stories Press, 1997.

Steinberg, David I. *Burma/Myanmar: What Everyone Needs to Know*. New York: Oxford University Press, 2010.

Wintle, Justin. *Perfect Hostage: A Life of Aung San Suu Kyi, Burma's Prisoner of Conscience*. New York: Skyhorse Publishing, 2007.

UPRISING IN EGYPT

Economist, "The Autumn of the Patriarchs," "The Awakening," February 19–25, 2011.

Economist, "An End or a Beginning?" February 5–11, 2011.

Economist, "The Long Standoff," February 12–18, 2011.

Economist, "Protest in Egypt: Another Arab Regime under Threat," January 29–February 4, 2011.

Kirkpatrick, David D., "Egyptians Defiant as Military Does Little to Quash Protests." *New York Times*, January 29, 2011. www.nytimes.com/2011/01/30/world/middleeast.

New York Times, "Egypt News: The Protests of 2011," "Egypt News: Revolution and Aftermath." topics.nytimes.com/top/news/international/countriesandterritories/Egypt.

Reuters, "Factbox: Quotes from Egyptians on Revolution," February 12, 2011. www.reuters.com.

IMAGE CREDITS

INDEX